"Matt Papa cares about the glory of G
that zeal on every page of this dynami
about you and me getting to grips with that glory. Sometimes
as preacher, sometimes as prophet, sometimes as pastor, Matt
guides us through these pages with kindness, seriousness, and
love—for God's greater glory and our greater good."

—Matt Redman, songwriter and worship leader

"Making our lives about one unflinching gaze upon the glory of
Christ—what a vision Matt Papa has put before us. I encourage
everyone—Christian and non-Christian alike—to take up and
read this book! We were all made to worship. The only question is
whom or what do we worship? Matt shows us the biblical answer,
and gives us compelling reasons for putting our eyes on Him."

—Tony Merida, pastor, professor, and author

"Matt Papa's book is a snakebite kit for suffering sinners. Each
sentence of *Look and Live* extracts Satan's deadly venom and re-
suscitates the soul with the life-giving power of the glory of God!"

—Tony Nolan, snakebite survivor, author,
and gospel preacher

"I have enjoyed the privilege of serving with Matt Papa numerous times, and have always sensed that his leadership was an
open invitation to join him in declarative worship. *Look and
Live* is pen to paper in what I have observed from Matt's life and
influence. To journey through this book is to go on a quest that
will awaken our souls to the reality of the One who is 'majestic
in holiness' and 'awesome in glorious deeds.'"

—Dr. Brent Crowe, author, speaker, and vice president
of Student Leadership University

"I am a Matt Papa fan, and have been wonderfully blessed by
his friendship and ministry. I am grateful his reflections on worship are now shared in writing in *Look and Live*. It is biblically
faithful and keeps the focus of worship where it belongs: on
our glorious God."

—Daniel L. Akin, president of Southeastern
Baptist Theological Seminary

"Whether in songs that help the church sing, or with words that aid us as we read, Matt Papa faithfully points us to the soul-stirring glory of God. Read this book and allow your heart to once again behold the wondrous mystery."

—Matt Boswell, founder of Doxology & Theology
and pastor of ministries and worship
at Providence Church, Frisco, Texas

"I've worked with Matt for years as we attempt to proclaim the gospel of Jesus Christ. Matt's always been a thoughtful and passionate minister, but he seems to have tapped into something deeply powerful in the pages of *Look and Live*. This is Matt's life message—that Jesus Christ alone is worth living for, and that when you gaze upon His majesty and glory you will never be the same. This book is theologically robust and practically helpful, packed with Scripture and insight into the person and work of the risen Son of God. Matt lives out this message as a dad, husband, worship leader, and evangelist. This is a true gift to the church and the world."

—Clayton King, president of Crossroads Camps
and Clayton King Ministries and teaching pastor
at NewSpring Church, South Carolina

"If C. S. Lewis and David Crowder wrote a book together about worship, you would have the rich theology of the great Christian apologist with the deep passion of worship from the contemporary artist. That's what Matt Papa has given us in *Look and Live*—a must-read for every worshiper."

—Mike Harland, president of LifeWay Worship

"Matt Papa's helpful book offers a compelling reminder that in the fast pace of life, there is a still small voice with a Galilean accent calling us to look and live: because He alone is the way, the truth, and the life."

—Dan DeWitt, author of *Jesus or Nothing* and dean
of Boyce College, undergraduate school
of The Southern Baptist Theological Seminary

LOOK
and
LIVE

BEHOLD THE SOUL-THRILLING,
SIN-DESTROYING **GLORY OF CHRIST**

MATT PAPA

BETHANY HOUSE PUBLISHERS
a division of Baker Publishing Group
Minneapolis, Minnesota

Published by Bethany House Publishers
11400 Hampshire Avenue South
Bloomington, Minnesota 55438
www.bethanyhouse.com

Bethany House Publishers is a division of
Baker Publishing Group, Grand Rapids, Michigan

Printed in the United States of America

Library of Congress Cataloging-in-Publication Data
Papa, Matt.
    Look and live : behold the soul-thrilling, sin-destroying glory of Christ / Matt Papa.
        pages cm
    Includes bibliographical references.
    Summary: "Worship leader and speaker shows that people's lives follow what their hearts focus on—whether the glory of God or themselves and their desires"— Provided by publisher.
    ISBN 978-0-7642-1251-2 (pbk. : alk. paper)
    1. Spirituality—Christianity. 2. God (Christianity)—Knowableness. 3. God (Christianity)—Worship and love. 4. Idolatry. 5. Desire—Religious aspects— Christianity. I. Title.
    BV4501.3.P357 2014
    248.4—dc23   2014017778

Cover design by LOOK Design Studio

Author is represented by Wolgemuth & Associates

15   16   17   18   19   20   21   9 8 7 6 5 4 3

This book is dedicated to
the precious people
of The Summit Church
in Durham, North Carolina.

It has been an honor to behold
the Lamb with you.

Contents

Acknowledgments

On a theoretical level, this book's existence is owing to the teaching, preaching, and writing ministries of the following pastor-theologians: Jonathan Edwards, John Piper, Tim Keller, and J.D. Greear.

Edwards' philosophical theology has been unparalleled in helping me see the world with "God glasses." I think Edwards' life was, in a sense, an exposition of the Isaiah 6 truth: "The whole earth is full of His glory."

John Piper's Christian hedonism has been crucial in helping me make the connections between worship and joy. Psalm 67 jumps into mind when I think about Dr. Piper: "Let the nations be glad and sing for joy. . . . Let the peoples praise You, O God; Let all the peoples praise You." Glory, joy, worship, mission . . . these contributions from Piper into my thinking have been profound and life-altering.

Tim Keller's astute and pastoral ability to take lofty theological concepts and make them bear down on the heart is, to my limited knowledge, unequaled. The phrase "full of grace and truth" comes to mind when I think of Dr. Keller. His preaching has been personally transforming, and this book owes a great debt to his ministry.

J.D. Greear, my pastor, has been a dear friend, and sitting under his teaching has uniquely helped me to make the connections between glory, the gospel, and true transformation. "We love, because He loved us first" are words that come to mind when I think of J.D. and his distinct contribution. I am truly grateful for all of these men, and I hope I have honored them with this work.

On a practical level, I would love to thank Bethany House Publishers for making this book a reality. I'm not sure if this is stereotypical to say in an acknowledgments section, because I've never done this before (writing a book), which is precisely why I am so grateful to them. They took a chance with me, and I see it as a gift . . . a bright scattered beam.

Finally, I would like to acknowledge the three gentlemen I affectionately call "my band": Zach Smith, Tyler Mount, and Jon Dobberstein. These dear friends and partners in ministry have walked with me through a lot. I distinctly remember a van ride about three years ago during which the (seven-hour) topic of conversation was "What is glory?" (I know. We are nerds.) Virtually every idea you will read in this book I have said on a stage somewhere, or in a van somewhere, with hours on end of follow-up discussion about accuracy, precision, and helpfulness with these men of God. This book started a long time ago. The van rides I think will always be my favorite memories. Scattered beams.

Foreword

"Bro, that makes me want to run through a wall." That's what Matt Papa said to me after we had spent an hour discussing the glory of Jesus revealed in and through the book of Revelation, and it pretty well summarizes Matt's life. When I listen to Matt teach about or lead worship, I feel like I'm watching a guy who has caught a glimpse of something glorious trying to run through a wall. And he makes me want to go with him.

I honestly don't know of anyone who has taught me more about worship than Matt Papa. For many years as a professional Christian I struggled to really love God. I knew a lot of facts about God, I was obedient in the church, and I knew how to engage fervently in mission, but the passions of my heart burned only lukewarm. Matt has helped me to see that love for God grows out of an experience of beholding the love of God. We burn only as we behold. The cross, as Matt loves to repeat, is the blazing center of the glory of God. So look, Matt says, and live.

Matt's worship shows us that true worship begins with the gospel and ends in the mission. It is a rhythm of revelation and response: beholding the wondrous mystery and declaring that mystery to others. It's what we see in Isaiah: God shows us His glory; we cover our faces and say, "Surely I am a man of unclean lips" and "here am I, send me." True worship never needs to be compelled. It is the natural response to seeing Something altogether glorious. True worship is simply glory reflecting off of our faces. It puts the value of the One we've just seen on display.

I believe Matt is the greatest songwriter of our generation. I know of no one who better grounds worship in the gospel or more passionately connects it to the mission. When I listen to his music I know that he has beheld something I want to behold. I want to follow him as he runs through a wall.

This is a fantastic book and I commend it to you with the most enthusiastic support. It will help pastors and worship leaders get a better grasp on how and why we worship, and how to teach that to others. It will help ordinary believers rediscover that Beauty calls for our most fervent acts of devotion. And it will help those who haven't yet been convinced of the Christian faith to catch a glimpse of that glorious sight that has so captivated saints through history and empowered its beholders to do the most remarkable things.

So don't just read this book, meditate your way through it. I'll warn you, however—you may want to put on a helmet first, because at some point in this book you're probably going to try to run through a wall.

J.D. Greear
Author of *Stop Asking Jesus Into Your Heart:*
How to Know for Sure You Are Saved

Introduction

Let me begin by saying this: This is a book about worship, and I am an expert on worship. I'm not being arrogant. It's just true.

You are an expert on worship, too.

Neurologist Daniel Levitin says, "Ten thousand hours of practice is required to achieve the level of mastery associated with being a world-class expert—in anything."[1] This would mean that at the ripe age of fourteen months, you became a worship expert.

It's all we do.

What we perceive to be just "life happening" . . . is not. It is the pulse of worship. The shrapnel of worship. The blast site of worship. Life is just picking up the pieces.

We are all facing *some* deity. Some glory has swept us off our feet, and this very moment, like a rabid animal, we are pursuing it. That's what life is.

My hope in these pages is that I can help you sense what is stirring down there in your soul. To feel what is happening. To remember it . . . like when you begin to recall a dream in the early morning after you wake. The soul is on a quest.

And then, ultimately, to help you know what to do with it. To know where to aim it. To its proper Object. That's what this book's about.

Let me also begin by saying this: I am *not* an expert on worship. As I write this, I am thirty years old. I'm not a doctor of anything. Really. I'm just a guy who likes to write and talk and sing. But I do love God. I adore Him. And even though on a visit to Rome you would probably be most helped by a really intelligent tour guide, maybe you could also be helped, if even a little, by the kid in the back saying, "Wow."

"Look!"

Maybe the kid will spark a little wonder in you.

"Behold, the Lamb of God who takes away the sin of the world!"

That's what I hope this book is for you. That's what I hope I am for you: a John the Baptist, the voice of one crying in the wilderness.[2]

"I thank the Lord if He makes my writings useful," John Newton once wrote. "I hope they contain some of His truths; and truth, like a torch, may be seen by its own light, without reference to the hand that holds it."[3]

Here's hoping you see the torch. The truth. The glory.

As fallen human beings we are plagued with inordinate affections. We love green pieces of paper more than God. We love balls made out of pigskin more than God. We've shown we even love apples more than God. We, like Esau, have traded our birthright—the dignity of our shameless, joy-filled, glory-beholding, glory-reflecting existence—for a bowl of beans.

As Blaise Pascal so aptly put, "Man's sensitivity to little things and insensitivity to the greatest things are marks of a strange disorder."[4] Our hearts are sensitive toward the little opinions of others, and insensitive to the great judgments of God.

And so, we worship our way into sin. We must worship our way out.[5]

We don't need more willpower. We don't need to get ourselves together. We need a greater thrill . . . a more captivating beauty.

What we need is a vision of God.

We need to see glory.

Are you addicted? Anxious? Unhappy? Still fighting that sin you've been fighting for years? Exhausted from trying harder? From religion?

I do not call you to work or to strive, but to simply lift up your eyes. *"Behold, the Lamb of God who takes away the sin of the world!"*

My aim is to help you overcome idolatry and certain sadness by pointing you to the all-satisfying, sin-destroying glory of Jesus.

Pointing being the key word.

This is not a book *on* God's glory. There isn't enough paper in the world or words in language to adequately do that.

The call is this: Make your life one unflinching gaze upon the glory of Christ.

Do this, and you will live.

Do not do this, and you will die. You will *die*.

You won't have victory over sin. You won't make it through your struggle.

You will tinker with toys and technology and all manner of counterfeit beauty until your life is wasted.

Look and Live!

The title of this book, *Look and Live*, comes from a familiar story in the Old Testament in Numbers 21. God's people were wandering through the wilderness. They became grouchy (as we do, too, when in the wilderness). Tired and hungry . . . grown-up kids who needed a nap.

They had eaten manna for a while now, and they were getting sick of it. Bamanna bread, mannacotti, manna burgers (shout-out to Keith Green). So they began whining. Grumbling. Disbelieving that their all-knowing Father knew what they needed.

Never a good idea.

Insulted by their unbelief and ingratitude, the Father gave them a spanking in the form of reptiles. God sent poisonous snakes to bite the people, and many of them began dying immediately. Naturally, as they often did (and we do, too, when our unbelief bites us), they returned and pleaded for mercy. The great intercessor Moses came to God and prayed for them, and God answered . . . in a rather interesting way:

> Then the Lord said to Moses, "Make a fiery serpent, and set it on a standard; and it shall come about, that everyone who is bitten, when he looks at it, he will live."
>
> Numbers 21:8

Thanks, Lord, but really?

Put a snake on a pole. That's what's going to rescue us?

Why show mercy in this way? Couldn't God have just made the snakes vanish? Or maybe turned them into cute little puppies? Why the snake-pole?

Jesus explains why in the two verses that precede the most well-known verse in all of the Bible:

> As Moses lifted up the serpent in the wilderness, even so must the Son of Man be lifted up; so that whoever believes in Him will have eternal life.
>
> John 3:14–15

God, the Father and Master-Teacher, orchestrated that moment in history—a true historical parable—to show us what the cross is about and what faith is like.

Faith is a looking.

It is the serious looking of sin-stricken, snake-bitten people toward God's peculiar and radical display of mercy . . . the crucified, bloody, exalted Son of God.

And if we don't see Him, we die.

We die.

We go to hell.

We have no victory over sin. Our lives remain a self-destructive mess. We have no joy. We are slaves to our addictions.

Unless we see Him. Unless we run to survey the Savior on the pole. Unless we fight through the crowds and through our doubts, and lift up our eyes.

The poison of idolatry will rot our veins until the glory of the crucified God-man permeates our vision. To live is to behold Him.

My call is not "Look and get a better life" or "Look and get a warm fuzzy."

From one who bears the fang-shaped scar, my call to you is: Behold the antivenom of the soul . . . the glory of God in the face of Jesus Christ.

Look and live.

1

Glory and Worship

The centre of me is always and eternally a terrible pain—a curious wild pain—a searching for something beyond what the world contains, something transfigured and infinite—the beatific vision—God—I do not find it, I do not think it is to be found—but the love of it is my life.

Bertrand Russell, 1916, Letter to Constance Malleson,
The Autobiography of Bertrand Russell

For something brighter than the
Glory of my name in the lights
For something truer than this
Got-it-all-together disguise
I've got this cry deep inside
There's got to be
Something bigger than me

"Bigger Than Me"
from the *Look & Live* album

I think I always knew what "glory" was, but only in the way most human beings know what it is, in a distant, haunted, indefinable kind of way.

19

I had seen glimpses of it in sports, heard its echoes in music, felt its charm in romance, and tasted its promise in success.

I even knew, growing up as a church kid, that God "had" lots of glory, but I couldn't really tell you why or how. I knew God was glorious much like the way a man who has never used a hammer "knows" the Burj Khalifa (the tallest building in the world) was difficult to build.

Of course it was. But what does he *know*?

The great theologian Jonathan Edwards described this kind of knowing well when he said, "There is a difference between having a rational judgment that honey is sweet, and having a sense of its sweetness."[1] The former, I believe, was my kind of knowledge of the most important reality in the world . . . the glory of God.

I knew it was there, but I didn't love that it was there.

I believed it, but I never beheld it.

I could recite it, but I couldn't relish it.

James speaks candidly about this sort of knowing: "You believe that there is one God. Good! Even the demons believe that—and shudder" (2:19 NIV). In other words, there is a kind of knowing—a cold, heartless kind—that is pointless, even demonic.

I grew up in the Bible Belt, and when you are in church every night of the week because that's what you do, your knowledge of God can become worse than demonic, because you forfeit the ability to do the one virtuous thing demons do: shudder.

Familiarity breeds apathy.

I was swimming in glory—surrounded by its sights and sounds—and my jaw was not on the floor where it should have been. I was rich but lived as a poor man, a guest to a feast but always hungry, like a man content to stare at stick figures while the *Mona Lisa* sits in his basement. I was too busy for Treasure. Too busy for Beauty.

Or so it seems looking back. Perhaps it will always be this way, remembering our faith of yesterday. The more you taste and see the magnificence of God in the now, the more you wonder if you were even a Christian five years ago.

After college I went into full-time ministry. Me and the sizable chip on my shoulder were ready and determined to change the world. God needed me on His team, and I was sure I would be the one to do something great and give the devil a definitive deathblow. (Yeah, I know, Somebody already did that. But when you're running around building a kingdom, sometimes you forget.)

God was certainly using me in wonderful ways. I was going on mission trips. I was leading Bible studies. I was doing loads of Christian things. My schedule was full, and it seemed that lots of people respected me. All the while, I was depressed, enslaved to the approval of others, and addicted to pornography.

I would love to tell you that today I stand "cured" of these things, but I'm not. I have been radically changed, and these wounds of mine, these diseases that I thought might bury me, have been tremendously healed. But I'm not "fixed." I'm still longing for the cure—that final, blessed remedy that happily waits in one place—the glory on His face. Until then, it's all-out war. I can say, however, that today, by God's grace, I'm standing. I'm in the fight, and I am living in victory. I'm generally content and at peace. From lust's powerful bonds I've been released. God has truly done a miraculous work in my life. My scars are numerous, my flesh is powerless, my enemy is dangerous, but my God is glorious and His grace is totally sufficient.

So what brought about the change?

Well, I'd like to say it was sheer willpower, 100-percent human grit and determination. There may have been an ounce of that, but it definitely wasn't that.

It wasn't by trying harder. It wasn't by my ability to say "no."

I didn't find victory by praying five hours every morning and fasting five days a week (although that would've been wonderful).

It wasn't the anti-porn computer software programs that I used on all of my computers that broke my addiction to pornography.

It wasn't all the accountability groups I was in.

These things all seemed to help me, but only on a kind of surface level. I was still sick, still dissatisfied, still *looking*.

The change came, but it was only by experiencing a greater Thrill. It was by beholding a greater Beauty. God.

I had a mentor ask me if I had simply been spending time with Jesus. Sadly the answer was no, so I began to set my own gaze on His glory, before I even knew what Glory was.

I began to look deeply into the gospel. Deeply into God's Word. Deeply into the cross.

I began to just sit with God—to seek Him in His temple (Psalm 27:4). And as I did this, slowly, something started happening.

Beauty began coming into view. A Light. A Brightness . . . which was there all along. I just had to let my eyes adjust. Now, an eclipse was occurring in my soul—a displacing of all counterfeit beauty and lesser thrills.

I began to taste the sweetness of the Honey.

I began to tremble, to smile, in the most self-forgetful way.

My whole being leaned toward this Eternal Weight. Everything inside of me was screaming, "I was made for this!" There was Substance.

I was seeing God, the Glory I was created for. And I knew in that moment, in my bones, what it would mean for me to choose to fix my soul-gaze upon this Beauty. It was clear what the result would be.

Life.

Transversely, I understood in that moment the consequence of choosing to look away. I knew the result of going back, back to the numbness, back to the short-lived, candy-coated, one-night-stand idols I had once adored.

Back to gulping from the empty, ever-deepening wells of wealth and pornography.

I knew the consequence of throwing the full weight of my inconsolable soul onto the shadows of this creation.

Disillusionment. Disappointment. Despair.

I knew in that moment the consequence of turning away from this matchless Glory . . . of looking back.

Pillar of salt.

Death.

The change didn't happen overnight. It occurred over about a three-year period of regularly setting my eyes toward God. But as Beauty began coming into view, I began to feel something I had never felt before. A satisfaction, an incomparable thrill, and a displacing of all lesser ones.

Suddenly, sin wasn't as sweet anymore. Like being offered a McRib sandwich after I enjoyed a filet mignon.

I got a glimpse of Glory, and I was changed. Forever set on a trajectory of seeking more of these Glory-glimpses.

I looked, and I lived.

The Quest of the Soul

I discovered that I was not alone in my hunt for glory, something more than myself. It has been going on since time began.

Sehnsucht.

That's right. Sehnsucht (pronounced zeyn-zookht). Don't blame me. Blame twentieth-century British author C. S. Lewis, who wrote about it in his book *Surprised by Joy.*

Sehnsucht is a German word that is hard to translate directly. It is made up of three words:

Sehn (to long for, to sigh, to yearn, to desire, to miss),

Sehen (to see, to view, to watch, or to behold), and

Sucht (a mania, an addiction, an obsession).

In other words, Sehnsucht describes the deep desire that exists in all of us like a throbbing obsession.

It is the soul's aching addiction to see Glory.

It is the soul's cry: More!

It is that feeling we all know—that sensation awakened by viewing a beautiful sunset, by watching an underdog's comeback victory.

Sehnsucht, that sleeping hungry giant, is awakened by and hungry for *glory*.

My aim in these pages, my hope by the Holy Spirit, is to awaken a giant in you. To revive a glory-hungry giant and then point it to its proper and necessary Object. To point it away from the empty wells that cannot satisfy and toward the Fountain of infinite satisfaction.

Whenever we place Sehnsucht on any created thing, the thing is devoured and the soul is disappointed. The insatiable must have the Inexhaustible. The inconsolable must have the Incomparable.

We were made for only one glory. One glory that Sehnsucht cannot consume. One glory that is enough.

The glory of God.

The Grammar of Glory

If someone asked you, "What is glory?" what would you say?

Many would respond in nebulous, romantic, confusing speech, even though the term is somewhat common Christian vocabulary.

Glory is difficult to define for two reasons.

First, it is difficult because it is so similar to the word *beauty*. Beauty is something we all recognize immediately when we see it, but something we can scarcely give parameters in a definition. It is something transcendent that we experience—some pleasing quality that demands our attention, found in a thousand places. Glory is very similar. We know it when we see it. It is a word befitting poetry . . . and Deity.

Second, *glory* is difficult to grasp because of its broad uses in the Bible. *Glory* (and its word-kins) appears in the Scriptures as a noun, a verb, an adjective, an adverb, and the object of prepositions. Think about these various uses of the word *glory* in the Bible:

Worthy are You, our Lord and our God, to receive glory. (Revelation 4:11)

Then Moses said, "I pray You, show me Your glory!" (Exodus 33:18)

Whether, then, you eat or drink or whatever you do, do all to the glory of God. (1 Corinthians 10:31)

. . . looking for the blessed hope and the appearing of the glory of our great God and Savior, Christ Jesus. (Titus 2:13)

Therefore in the east give glory to the Lord; exalt the name of the Lord. (Isaiah 24:15 NIV)

Awake, my glory! Awake, harp and lyre! I will awaken the dawn. (Psalm 57:8)

When Christ, who is our life, is revealed, then you also will be revealed with Him in glory. (Colossians 3:4)

But You, O Lord, are a shield about me, My glory, and the One who lifts my head. (Psalm 3:3)

But God forbid that I should glory, save in the cross of our Lord Jesus Christ. (Galatians 6:14 KJV)

So glory is something that God *has*? Maybe something God *is*? And it's something that we give *to* God? Like praise or something? And it's a *place* that I'm going to go one day?

Yes.

Confused? Me too.

But don't be discouraged. This great scope of uses for the word *glory* is perhaps just another reason it is wonderful to ascribe to our great God.

The word *glory* appears in Scripture most commonly in two ways.

First, in its most recurring sense, *glory* occurs as a noun, as some adorning quality that something or someone possesses (e.g., the glory of God in Exodus 33:18 and Titus 2:13). For practical purposes, let's call this *glory-within.*

Second, it most often appears as a kind of response of worship to something or someone, which can take the form of a noun or a verb (e.g., glory to God, to God be glory, or glorify God in Revelation 4:11 and Isaiah 24:15). Let's call this *glory-given.*

The business of this book is to examine glory-within and to understand its relevance to God and to our lives. *Relevance* being the key word. Greater knowledge of God is useless if it is not for the greater worship of God.

Stay with me.

Let me show you three biblical puzzle pieces that fit together to fully explain glory-within.

Biblical puzzle piece #1: The most common Hebrew word for glory is *kabowd* (pronounced kaw-bode). It means "honor, dignity, splendor, or abundance." More clarifying, though, is the root form of this word, which is *kabad* (pronounced kaw-bad). Kabad essentially means "weight," the heaviness or the weight of something or someone.

With respect to God, then, the glory of God would be God's weightiness—His infinite importance and value.

Biblical puzzle piece #2: The Scriptures teach us that glory is in a multitude of places and things, and exists in varying degrees. For example, there's the glory of fruitfulness (Isaiah 35:2), the glory of the land (Ezekiel 25:9), and the glory of horses (Job 39:20 KJV).

Then there's the glory of men and women individually (1 Corinthians 11:7), the glory of Solomon (Matthew 6:29), the glory of the church (Ephesians 5:27), the glory of angels (Hebrews 9:5), and, of course, there is that which is above all, over all, the Source of it all and the point of it all . . . the glory of God.

So, if we, like good puzzle enthusiasts, combine puzzle pieces 1 and 2, it would seem that all things exist with some degree of weight, value, or importance. A tree or a dog might possess glory—some degree of worth or value—simply because it exists. But the glory of a tree is certainly less than the glory of a man, since man is crowned by God with glory (Psalm 8:5) and made in His very image and likeness (Genesis 1:27). Similarly, the glory of a man—his importance or dignity—is infinitely less than the glory of the God who created him.

It would seem that a thing's sheer existence is a display of its glory, its worth, for if it had *no value* it should not exist at all.[2] However, we should not say that *all* things exist with glory, for many of the things that mankind creates do not possess goodness, because mankind is fallen. Therefore, it follows to say that all things, or actions, possess glory to the degree that they are a reflection of the glory of God.

Do you have a puzzle headache yet? Just one more piece.

Biblical puzzle piece #3: The *goodness* of something seems to be an important aspect of glory, especially in light of Exodus 33.[3]

When Moses said to God that greatest of prayers—"Show me Your glory"—God's response was, "I Myself will make all My goodness pass before you." It seems that perhaps the goodness of God *is* His glory. Or, as Charles Spurgeon said, "The brightest gem in the crown of God's glory is His goodness."[4]

So, now we combine all these puzzle pieces. And glory-defined appears. As Jonathan Edwards said, "Glory is the outshining of internal excellence."[5]

Glory. The weight of intrinsic goodness. The manifest gravity of dignity.

From Glory to Worship

Now let's move on to what I call *glory-given* (i.e., "glory to God").

Glory-given is the reverence of glory-within.

To glorify something is to say, "Wow! This is *good*. Everyone look!" This is the way that *glory* most often appears in the New Testament. It is the Greek word *doxa*. Glory-given.

Worship.

Perhaps you have heard some of the common Christian buzz phrases:

"You were made to worship."
"Worship is a lifestyle."
"Worship is more than a song."

I certainly would not disagree with them. We are all worshipers. However, these phrases are wimpy in their power to communicate the truth of our condition. Worship is not merely a lifestyle choice.

We cannot not *worship.*

In 2005, New England Patriots quarterback Tom Brady was interviewed by Steve Kroft of *60 Minutes*. At one point in the interview, Brady said:

> Why do I have three Super Bowl rings, and still think there's something greater out there for me? I mean, maybe a lot of people would say, "Hey man, this is what is." I reached my goal, my dream, my life. Me, I think: God, it's gotta be more than this. I mean, this can't be what it's all cracked up to be. I mean, I've done it. I'm 27. And what else is there for me?[6]

Brady was already one of the most decorated QBs of all time. Three Super Bowls. Hall of Fame stats. Television ads. Ladies love him. And he wanted *more*?

What was he after? What did he want?

In Exodus 32, God's people find themselves in a similar situation.

Feet tapping. Getting restless.

Israel had just seen the fireworks of the exodus . . . the giant walls of water and the plagues and the drowning armies. They had just experienced the terrifying thunder and lightning of Sinai. They had seen God's hand and mighty outstretched arm. But now, suddenly, it's as if they forgot it all.

> When the people saw that Moses delayed to come down from the mountain, the people assembled about Aaron and said to him, "Come, make us a god who will go before us; as for this Moses, the man who brought us up from the land of Egypt, we do not know what has become of him." Aaron said to them, "Tear off the gold rings which are in the ears of your wives, your sons, and your daughters, and bring them to me." Then all the people tore off the gold rings which were in their ears and brought them to Aaron. He took this from their hand, and fashioned it with a graving tool and made it into a molten calf; and they said, "This is your god, O Israel, who brought you up from the land of Egypt."
>
> Exodus 32:1–4

Now, many times we give Aaron and God's people a hard time here.

I mean, come on, guys . . . a gold cow? Really?!? After all the smoke and pyrotechnics of the exodus?

But what I want to point out is not the stupidity but the craving—the hunger. Moses really wasn't up there that long, but look . . . *the people are bored.* They are getting busy.

It's almost as if they *need* something to worship.

And this is the truest condition of our souls. You see, it is not merely that "we are worshipers" or merely that "worship is a lifestyle." That is far too weak.

We cannot not *worship.*

We are worship machines.

Pascal called it our propensity to "diversion." Augustine used the word *restless.* Edwards used the word *disposition.* Call it what you want, but we are continually bowing down to our highest perceived beauty. We are obsessed. Addicted. All of us, addicted to something.

The question is, to what?

Tim Keller, in his book *Encounters with Jesus*, tells how American writer David Foster Wallace articulated this idea perfectly in a commencement speech to the graduating class of Kenyon College in 2005:

> Everybody worships. The only choice we get is what to worship. And the compelling reason for maybe choosing some sort of god . . . to worship . . . is that pretty much anything else you worship will eat you alive. If you worship money and things, if they are where you tap real meaning in life, then you will never have enough, never feel you have enough. . . . Worship your own body and beauty and sexual allure, and you will always feel ugly. . . . Worship power, and you will end up feeling weak and afraid, and you will need ever more power over others to numb you to your own fear. Worship your intellect, being seen as smart, you will end up feeling stupid, a fraud, always on the verge of being found out. Look, the insidious thing about these forms of worship is not that they are evil or sinful; it is that they're unconscious. They are default settings.

Not even a religious person, Wallace understood that everyone worships. Everyone builds their life on something. Sadly, two years after giving that speech, Wallace committed suicide.[7]

Do you see? Something is going to eat you alive. "When we sin, worship does not stop," Harold Best says. "It changes directions."[8]

We never begin worship. We aim it.

The crucial question is: *What* do you worship?

And closely connected to that question is another question: *Why* are we always worshiping?

Worship, like love or faith, is a response.

As pastor David Platt says, "Worship is a rhythm of revelation and response."[9] You see something magnificent, and then respond in the praise or adoration of that thing. That's worship.

You behold or experience some glory, whether it's the glory of a slam dunk, the glory of a sunset, the glory of a rock band, or the glory of God, and then, quite naturally, you overflow with awe.

You sing. You say "Wow!" You call others to experience it with you.

Are you beginning to see the relationship between glory and worship? Worship is offering *glory-given* in response to seeing *glory-within*.

It is giving value to whatever we see to be valuable.

We worship whatever we enjoy and respect most. This is why the glory vision is always before the worship expression—the way that eating the filet mignon happens before the "Mmm," the way the touchdown happens before the eruption of applause.

Glory entices and "begins" worship. The vision of glory is where the journey of worship starts. The reason we are always worshiping is because we are always looking at something. And sometimes the glory appears so great, so massive, so important, you will sacrifice whatever it takes to get it.

This is why, after being a worship leader for fifteen years, I have chosen to focus on the topic of glory rather than worship. Worship is the natural by-product of seeing glory. Glory is foundational to worship. And if I can point just a few eyes to the glory of Jesus in these pages, songs of worship and lives of praise will rise unending to my glorious King.

The Crushing Weight of Glory

When the US stock market crashed in 2008, the chief financial officer of Freddie Mac hanged himself in his basement. A French money manager who invested many of Europe's leading families' money lost over a billion dollars, so he slit his wrists and died in his Madison Avenue office.

What happened? Their god got crucified. These people set their gaze on the glory of wealth. They invested their entire lives, their wallets, their family's wallets, and their businesses into something that was never strong enough or stable enough to merit that kind of investment. They gave money too much weight, too much glory. We see the same story in Scripture in Luke 12:16–20:

> And He told them a parable, saying, "The land of a rich man was very productive. And he began reasoning to himself, saying, 'What shall I do, since I have no place to store my crops?' Then he said, 'This is what I will do: I will tear down my barns and build larger ones, and there I will store all my grain and my goods. And I will say to my soul, "Soul, you have many goods laid up for many years to come; take your ease, eat, drink and be merry."' But God said to him, 'You fool! This very night your soul is required of you; and now who will own what you have prepared?'"

Crash.

This is the essence of sin, and the story of all our lives. We have all set our hopes onto something or someone we thought was really impressive and important. Something we thought would really make us happy . . . money, another person, a position. So we examine the thing. We lean on it a little bit. We test it. We taste it. It seems *good*. We respect it a little more, so we lean on it a little more. Pretty soon we trust enough to place the full weight of our soul upon it, and then . . . crash.

We end up disappointed. Despairing.

Why?

Because it wasn't God. And everything crumbles under the weight of worship except God.

When I had just graduated from college, I was beginning my pursuit of a career in Christian music. My band and I were playing a lot of places, and God was extremely gracious to provide us with lots of opportunities. However, I wasn't really happy, because I wasn't on a "label."

For me, getting a record deal was that next level of success I needed (it was my god). I was sure that when that happened,

I would be totally content and wouldn't live in white-knuckled anxiety anymore.

Well, guess what? It happened.

And I wasn't content.

On top of that, I was so exhausted from all the interviews, traveling, etc., to this place of "happiness" that I ended up in a depression!

That god just wasn't good enough. Sadly true in my life were the words of philosopher Ravi Zacharias: "The loneliest moment in life is when you have just experienced what you thought would deliver the ultimate—and it has let you down."[10]

The triune God is the only thing large enough and interesting enough to bear the weight of glory, and ultimately worship. Anything else will break your heart.

Money isn't secure enough.

Sex isn't thrilling enough.

Entertainment isn't impressive enough.

Music isn't interesting enough.

Food isn't satisfying enough.

People aren't reliable enough.

This world isn't good enough. Creation isn't permanent enough. We were created by God and for God, and until we understand that, we are restless, brokenhearted glory chasers, always seeking something more.

Only God, the highest and greatest good, the infinite holy One, is finally *enough*.

Where Do You Go for Glory?

Maybe you're having a great time living life the way you want to live it—spending your money where you want to spend it, using your time how you want to use it, setting your gaze on the glory that's around you—and you are perfectly happy and content with no God telling you how you should live.

Let me say this to you with all the love in my heart: Your crash is coming. It's called death.

Everything around you is passing. This life is a vapor. Don't wager your soul on a glory so small—this world and all of its beauty bluffs. Only the infinite God is enough. Don't gamble away your existence for stuff.

"For what does it profit a man to gain the whole world, and forfeit his soul?" (Mark 8:36).

So what do you worship? What "glory" are you looking at? Where is the whole attention of your soul? And most importantly, can the object of your worship bear the weight of worship?

Sometimes it is difficult to know what exactly we worship. Many of us would like to say "God," but many times our lives indicate otherwise.

Take some time now to prayerfully work through the following questions. Examine each one of them and ask God to lay your heart bare before Him. Write, if that helps you.

In your life, what achievement would finally make you happy? What one thing, if you lost it, would ultimately destroy your happiness? That is what you worship.

Where do you spend your time and your treasure? Our money and our time flow effortlessly to whatever our true god is.

What things typically make you angry? Anxious? Deeply depressed? Our emotions are like smoke from the fire of the altar of the true god we worship.

Turn to God. Now. Test Him. Try Him. See if He won't satisfy the depths of your soul.

Look to Him, really look. Linger long enough to let your eyes adjust.

See if He isn't as magnificent as what I can describe and more. Examine if He might be that treasure you are seeking—that deep-seated, death-defying satisfaction that you hunt like a throbbing obsession.

Labor to see Him, to know Him the way you have labored and sacrificed in service to your other gods. He will not disappoint.

As C. S. Lewis famously said, "If I find in myself a desire which no experience in this world can satisfy, the most probable explanation is that I was made for another world."[11]

Let us turn now to that world . . .

2

The Glory of God

The panorama of his perfections . . . is the end of our soul's quest for eternal satisfaction. He is infinite; and that answers to our longing for completeness. He is eternal; and that answers to our longing for permanence. He is unchangeable; and that answers to our longing for stability and security. There is none like God. Nothing can compare with him. Money, sex, power, popularity, conquest—nothing can compare with God.

John Piper

> Show me, show me, show me Your glory
> Oh, let your goodness come eclipse the world
> Show me, show me, show me Your glory
> I'm forever changed with just a glimpse, oh Lord
>
> "Show Me Your Glory"
> from the *Look & Live* album

Certain people in my youth group growing up, the super-spiritual ones, spoke often about "the glory of God." They would pray these long, elaborate (boring) prayers on the verge of incantation, saying things like, "Oh God, please let your glory fall! Glorify yourself in this place! We give you glory! Let your glory be revealed!"

Honestly, I thought it was all weird. Hooky spooky. Jesus-talk. I didn't understand it, and I was pretty sure a lot of them didn't either (*"Bless their hearts"*). So I dismissed it all—the jargon and preoccupation of the spiritual elite, mystics with their heads in the clouds. No earthly good.

And then I began to look . . . and live. And I began to see God's glory.

One of my favorite things to do in life is to watch human beings do the thing they are really good at—the thing they were "born to do." I love to watch videos of Michael Jordan making defenses look stupid. I love watching Yo-Yo Ma meticulously and effortlessly playing a Bach suite on the cello. I love watching my wife tirelessly raising our three little girls with an indomitable joy on her face.

I love watching dancers dancing, runners running, singers singing, chefs cooking, and comedians joking—doing the thing that, yes, they have worked hard at, but also what they were uniquely hardwired to do. It is beautiful. Their talent interlaced with their effort makes them simply in a class by themselves, and watching it is awesome, in the real sense of the word.

When we watch human beings do what they were made to do, we might say we are "seeing their glory," the outshining of internal excellence. Their excellence exudes from them for the world to admire. Their uniqueness.

The same is true with God.

When we look around the world, and more specifically, when we look in the Bible, we see the outshining of His internal excellence.

Imagine for a moment that you are a guitar player. Let's say playing guitar has been something that you have enjoyed doing for the last twenty years. You deeply pride yourself in your playing abilities and are considered by many in your peer group and in your community to be the best guitarist in your town.

One night, you are playing for a party. Everyone is having a good time and seems to be admiring your epic skills.

Then, as you're hanging out with the guests, shaking hands and high-fiving . . . suddenly Jimi Hendrix walks in.

What do you do?

You probably get a little quiet. You cower. You lose a sense of your self. You want to leave. Hide. Run.

Would you dare challenge him? Would you dare assert your excellence in the presence of his?

More likely you would forget about all your excellence and mutter, "I am ruined."

The glory of God is the reason why every person in the Bible who encounters God nearly falls dead. It changes you.

When we see God, we get small.

We lose a sense of our self.

We must.

His is true excellence. His is true glory. All would-be identities vanish like a shadow in the presence of I AM.

Pride cannot exist in His presence.

My aim in this chapter is simply to consider God with you. To consider just a few of his innumerable attributes and the glory we were made for. We will certainly not hit the "panorama of his perfections," as John Piper describes them, nor will all the books of the world, but we'll behold a few glimpses together.

Trying to Define It

Thus far we have defined "glory," but we have yet to define the "glory of God." If *glory* is the outshining of internal excellence, then we might easily say that the *glory of God* is the outshining of God's internal excellence. This is true, but as John Piper points out, we are helped a little more by a contrast we see in the Scriptures between the holiness of God and the glory of God.

In Isaiah chapter six, we see an awe-inspiring vision of the Lord. The angels are shaking the foundations of heaven with their voices, saying: "Holy, holy, holy, is the Lord Almighty . . . the whole earth is full of his _____" (v. 3 NIV).

You might think they would fill in that blank with the word *holiness*. But they don't. They fill it in with the word *glory*.[1] Why? I think this is why: The earth is the manifestation of God's goodness, mind, and excellence—His "outshining," you might say. It's what we can apprehend. What we can stomach.

We will never begin to perceive the infinite depths of God's mind and heart. This is God's holiness.

He is beyond.

And yet, He has revealed himself in ways that are beautiful, high, yet understandable in the world.

This is God's glory.

"His glory is the open revelation of the secret of his holiness," Piper says. "The holiness of God is His concealed glory. The glory of God is His revealed holiness."[2]

Holy, Holy, Holy

The holiness of God is an attribute of God that I am convinced has gotten a bad rap.

It is like the weird uncle of God's attributes . . . or the bitter old grandpa.

People say things like, "Yes, God is loving, kind, and gracious. But He is holy!"[3] As if to say, you better watch out, you better not cry, you better not pout I'm telling you why . . . God's holiness is coming to town!

I can remember growing up in church and having people tell me that I needed to fear God because God is holy. I never understood this, because I was always told that *holy* meant "pure." I never understood why I needed to be scared of some morally perfect grandpa in the sky.

These views foundationally misunderstand God and the term *holy*.

The word *holy* in Hebrew means "separate." Set apart. A cut above. For something to be holy means that that thing is in a class by itself. It is other. There's nothing like it.

Think unique.

Beyond compare.

Matchless. Exceptional. Consummate.

Think secret.

Uncharted. Unexplored. Unfamiliar.

Mysterious. Alien.

> Who is like You among the gods, O Lord? Who is like You, majestic in *holiness*, Awesome in praises, working wonders?
>
> Exodus 15:11

God's holiness is not so much an attribute of God as it is the foundation of all his attributes. It is Him.

Think about it.

In Isaiah 6:3, the angels do not say, "Love, love, love . . ." although God is love. They do not say, "Wise, wise, wise . . ." although He is wise. They do not say, "Pure, pure, pure . . ."

They say, "Holy, holy, holy . . ." Why is this?

Because God is holy in every way. His love is a holy love. His wisdom is a holy wisdom. His power is a holy power. And this is why the angels never cease to say . . .

Holy.

I imagine them encircling His throne, covering their faces and their feet as they fly. They peek and see some quality of God, and they shout "Holy!" as they quickly hide their faces.

They peek again in curious wonder and see some other aspect of Him, and shout "Holy!"

Seeing and singing. Forever and ever . . . on and on and on.

You see, He is holy. In every way. In all of His attributes. He is in a class by himself.

An ocean without a shore. A mountain without a peak. And yet, this amazing Being has revealed himself. He has displayed His glory. He didn't have to. He could have remained in perpetual secrecy. Holy.

But He created a world.

He created you and me, and He doesn't treat us like toe jam. He treats us with dignity. He shows us what He is doing. He tells us about himself. He speaks to sinful, biblical authors in words they can understand and write down. He speaks to you and me. He was a Jewish carpenter.

Glory.

The Glory of the Trinity

The doctrine of the Trinity is simultaneously the most difficult and most beautiful of all the doctrines of Christianity. It has boggled the sharpest minds for centuries. Every metaphor falls flat. And yet the more you peer into it, the more it allures your attention, the more breathtaking it becomes, the more you see it as the foundation of all reality.

The word *Trinity* (not appearing in the Bible) is a theological label meant to summarize the teachings of certain passages of Scripture. (Other important theological terms that don't appear in Scripture, but that many Christians believe are taught in it, include *communion, incarnation, free will, rapture,* and *advent.*)

Even though it never uses the word *Trinity*, the Bible teaches us that *God is one God in three persons*: Father, Son, Holy Spirit.

He is not three Gods in three persons.

He is not one God with three different forms or phases.

He is one God in three persons, existing simultaneously and eternally. There is nothing in the universe like this.

Then God said, "Let us make man in our image, after our likeness."

Genesis 1:26 ESV

Who is He talking to? From the very beginning of time we see a plurality in God. God is One. And He is more than one. This boggles the mind.

But we must try.

For worship's sake (and somewhat for humor's sake), let's examine some of the most commonly used metaphors for the Trinity.

The Trinity Is Like an Egg

Some say the Trinity is like an egg (or a Blow Pop or three-leaf clover).

The egg has three distinct parts—the shell, the white, and the yolk—but it is one egg.

Makes sense, right? Or not.

Actually, the egg metaphor for God is an ancient heresy called Partialism, which states that the Father, Son, and Holy Spirit are not distinct persons of the Godhead, but rather different parts of God. Just as the shell of an egg is not fully an egg, each is one-third of God.

Dreadfully wrong.

Jesus is fully God.

The Trinity Is Like the Sun

Some say the Trinity is like the sun.

In the sun you have the star, you have the light that comes from the star, and then you have the heat, and yet they are all interconnected. Makes sense. Maybe?

Not so much.

This metaphor represents an ancient heresy called Arianism. In Arianism, Christ and the Holy Spirit (the light and the heat) are creations of the Father (the star) and not one in nature with Him. Because they are contingent beings, that would make only the Father God.

The Trinity Is Like Water

Some say the Trinity is like water.

Water is one thing, yet it can exist in three forms: solid, liquid, or gas.

This metaphor illustrates an ancient heresy called Modalism. In Modalism, God the Father "becomes" God the Son, and God the Son "becomes" God the Holy Spirit. God is one God who periodically changes forms or modes.

All of these explanations of the Trinity try, yet . . .

To be God means to be an eternal, all-knowing, sovereign, all-powerful being. To be a person means to be a distinct, unique center of thought, emotion, and will.

God is one essence or being, and three persons.

The Father is God. The Son is God. The Spirit is God. They are One.

Yet, the Father is not the Son. The Son is not the Spirit. And the Spirit is not the Father. There is a One-ness and a Three-ness.

The Father is totally God (John 6:27; Romans 1:7; 1 Peter 1:2) and yet has a distinct personhood and role within the Trinity (1 Corinthians 8:6; Revelation 4:11; John 3:16–17).

The Son is totally God (John 1:1; Colossians 2:9; Revelation 1:8; Hebrews 1:8) and yet has a distinct personhood and role within the Trinity (John 4:42; Matthew 11:27; 1 Corinthians 8:6).

The Holy Spirit is totally God (2 Corinthians 3:17; John 15:26; Acts 5:3–4) and yet has a distinct personhood and role within the Trinity (Genesis 1:2; Psalm 104:30; John 16:12–15; Acts 10:38).

Make sense?

"The Trinity's like an egg!"

No.

"It's like the sun!"

No.

"Like water!"

No.

It's not like anything. He's not like anything. He is holy.

Let's keep at it. Are you with me?

Perhaps the greatest biblical text on the doctrine of the Trinity is this one: "God is love" (1 John 4:8).

What?

"There's nothing there about the Trinity," you might say.

But this is where we really begin to see the glistening beauty of this doctrine. While it is intellectually difficult (some might say impossible), from a practical and emotional standpoint, this doctrine is one of the most helpful and beautiful things in the universe.

If you ask Muslims, "Is your god a god of love?" They will say, "Yes, of course." If you ask them further, "Then who did he love before the foundation of the world?" They will have no answer. Because their god is one god in one person.

In the words "God is love," we find a declaration of the eternal plurality of the nature of God. He is love, because He is, in essence, a relationship. And it is a relationship like no other. In Tim Keller's book *The Reason for God,* he writes:

> The life of the Trinity is characterized not by self-centeredness but by mutually self-giving love. When we delight and serve someone else, we enter into a dynamic orbit around him or her, we center on the interests and desires of the other. That creates a dance, particularly if there are three persons, each of whom moves around the other two. So it is, the Bible tells us. Each of the divine persons centers upon the others. None demands that the others revolve around him. Each voluntarily circles the other two, pouring love, delight and adoration into them. Each person of the Trinity loves, adores, defers to and rejoices in the others.[4]

Keller then quotes C. S. Lewis:

In Christianity God is not an impersonal thing nor a static thing—not even just one person—but a dynamic pulsating activity, a life, a kind of drama, almost, if you will not think me irreverent, a kind of dance. . . . [The] great fountain of energy and beauty spurting up at the very centre of reality.[5]

We exist to look into that pulsating activity. We exist to be whisked up into that.

Addiction is really our war against the chasm that God left in us when we left Him. The stuff we put in there hasn't worked and it never will, because we were made for the embrace of the Trinity.

Only the Triune God is finally enough.

The Glory of I AM

On July 3, 1983, I was born. Nine months prior to that, I was conceived. Because of my parents' passion, and ultimately God's plan, on that day I became an eternal soul.

Effect.

Prior to that moment, I had no existence.

We can all relate to beginnings—"Once upon a time. . . ." We all had one of those. We can also relate to future forevers—"And they lived happily ever after . . ." because we will all have one of those. (We might not all necessarily have a "happy" ever after, but we will all have an ever after, nonetheless.)

Like God, we are all everlasting beings. And that is amazing. What we cannot relate to, however, is the endless abyss of eternity past. We cannot relate to the absolute, terrifying holiness of God's self-existence.

I AM.

He never had a beginning.

Never.

Think.

God is simply *there*.

Before the mountains were brought forth, or ever you had formed the earth and the world, from everlasting to everlasting you are God.

Psalm 90:2 ESV

Okay, so . . . where were you, God? What did you do?
"I AM."
Were you planning your future creation? For how long?
"I AM."

Then Moses said to God, "If I come to the people of Israel and say to them, 'The God of your fathers has sent me to you,' and they ask me, 'What is his name?' what shall I say to them?" God said to Moses, "I AM WHO I AM" And he said, "Say this to the people of Israel, 'I AM has sent me to you.'"

Exodus 3:13–14 ESV

Not an effect. God has no mommy or daddy. He's simply *there*.

What does this mean? It means that all the things in the universe—you, me, the book you are reading, the chair you are sitting in—are not as real as God.

We are contingency. He is Reality.

The entire cosmos—from the smallest ant to the greatest star—is like a dust mite compared to the weight of the mountain of God's I AM-ness. We are the shadow. He is the Substance. To doubt Him is insanity.

What else does this mean?

It means that God does not need anything, just as the artist does not need his latest painting. He may delight in it. It may have great value to him. But he does not need it. God, *the* Artist, does not need you, and this is a great cause to worship Him.

We spend so much energy trying to maintain the delusion that creation is permanent. This fuels all of our addiction, sin, and idolatry. We frolic through life trying to convince ourselves of it, but deep down we know it's not, and *that* is really why we are anxious.

One day we will all awaken from this dream called the universe, this dream called life, to the sheer reality of God's I AM-ness. And when we do—when you do—will your life have been built on the shadow or the substance? Will you have lived your life for "it was" or for "I AM"?

So I invite you, even if you have heard some of these things before, to gaze deeper into them, for that is why you exist.

The Glory of God's Power

Louis Cyr (1863–1912) was a famous French-Canadian strongman who is said by many to be the strongest man to ever live. At his peak, Louis was 5 feet 10 inches and weighed 310 pounds. He had a 21-inch neck, a 45-inch waist, 22-inch biceps, and 19-inch forearms.

Basically, the man was a square.

His résumé is quite stunning. It almost has the appearance of a tall tale, though it is historically attested. His feats include:

- Lifting a 500-pound weight with one finger
- Lifting a platform on his back, which held eighteen men and totaled 4,337 pounds
- At age nineteen, lifting a 514-pound rock from ground up to his shoulder
- Once resisting the pull of four draught horses, holding two in each hand, while grooms cracked their whips to make the horses pull harder[6]

Well, God's résumé is also quite impressive. His feats include:

- Louis Cyr
- the universe

Psalm 33:6–9 tells us:

> By the word of the Lord the heavens were made, and by *the breath of His mouth all their host. He gathers the waters of the sea together as a heap*; He lays up the deeps in storehouses. Let all the earth fear the Lord; let all the inhabitants of the world stand in awe of Him. *For He spoke, and it was done; He commanded, and it stood fast.*

God's power is a holy power. It is in a class by itself.
We pick up sticks. God picks up oceans.
We breathe out carbon dioxide. God breathes out stars.

One of the best places to see the glory of God is *up*. The Bible says "the heavens declare the glory of God" (Psalm 19:1 NIV). This means the skies are saying something. And that something is this: "God is massive, eternal, creative, powerful."
We should listen to them. Consider these fun space facts:

- You could fit one million earths inside our star, the sun.
- In a larger star named Betelguese, you could fit one billion (1,000,000,000) suns or 262 trillion (262,000,000,000,000) earths.
- The largest star in the universe is the VY Canis Majoris.
- It would take 9.3 billion (9,300,000,000,000) suns to fill Canis Majoris.
- It would take 11,666,192,832,000,000 earths to fill Canis Majoris.
- If Canis Majoris were put in our sun's place, it would extend past Saturn.

Feeling small yet?

- Try counting the stars. According to astronomers, there are anywhere from 100 to 400 billion stars in our Milky Way galaxy alone.

Or now?

- According to astronomers, there could be anywhere from 100 to 400 billion galaxies in the universe.
- The observable universe is somewhere around 47 billion light years in every direction.[7]

Why in the world would God make something so massive and wild?

Assuming we are the only life in this endless black (which I do), couldn't He have just made the earth, the moon, and the sun? Or perhaps even just the earth with some sort of self-illumination?

But no. He didn't.

He made a terrifying, endless, beautiful, unexplored, unexplorable abyss. He made an immeasurable, untamed ocean of mega stars, galaxies, quasars, and black holes in which we are a mere floating speck.

Why?

The heavens declare the glory of God.

The Artist must have wanted to tell us something about himself. He is the real terrifying, endless, beautiful, unexplored, unexplorable Abyss. He is the immeasurable, untamed Ocean of truth, wisdom, goodness, and light in which we are a mere floating speck.

Holy.

Do you remember the Tower of Babel story?

I love this story. Genesis 11 says the people had worked and labored and sweat for their own "name." Then "the Lord came down to see" what they had done.

He came *down* to see!

What an awesome backhand to all human glory and achievement.

A dedicated, energetic, intelligent person—or group of persons (as illustrated by the Tower of Babel)—can over the course of his or her lifetime create something great.

Just think . . . if we all got together today somewhere on our earth-speck and dedicated all our collective years of wisdom and strength, we could build ourselves a really nice, big building.

And God, with a word, spoke the cosmos.

> For all the gods of the peoples are idols,
> But the Lord made the heavens.
> Psalm 96:5

Glory.

We exist to celebrate, admire, hide in, and confide in something greater than ourselves. Someone stronger than ourselves.

Look around the world. We love to praise athletes, musicians, and actors who seem larger than life. The fact is, they are not, but we love to make them larger than life. And we get disappointed when they appear human. Why?

Because we were made for a God who is larger than life.

We were made to admire His power.

> The voice of the Lord is powerful,
> The voice of the Lord is majestic.
> The voice of the Lord breaks the cedars;
> Yes, the Lord breaks in pieces the cedars of Lebanon. . . .
> The voice of the Lord shakes the wilderness;
> The Lord shakes the wilderness of Kadesh.
> The voice of the Lord makes the deer to calve
> And strips the forests bare;
> And in His temple everything says, "Glory!"
> Psalm 29:4–5, 8–9

The Glory of God's Wisdom

One of the best places to see the glory of God is *in*. Human beings are incredible creations.

Genesis 1 tells us that God spent a day on the universe. He spent a full day on the land and all the hosts of varieties of grasses and plants and trees. It says the Artist used one full day to make the endless swarms of birds and ocean wildlife—tie-dyed fish and hammerhead sharks and giant blue whales and microscopic shrimp. He took one day to craft all the land-animal life. . . . from slow-moving cows to bowlegged grasshoppers to big-headed lions to kingdoms of ants.

Then, the great Artist spent another whole day on just one thing: A man.

Do you understand what an amazing creation you are? What wisdom is pulsing through your veins? Exuding from every square inch of your little frame?

God made us unique from all other creation. We are made in His image. And this means a lot of things:

We are intellectual.

We are emotional.

We are volitional.

We are relational.

We are spiritual.

We are creative.

We are everlasting.

We are souls uniquely made by God with distinctive gifts and tastes and nuances and desires, but all with a foundational, unending desire for His glory.

In an effort to display the wisdom of God, consider these amazing facts about the human body:

- 300 million cells die in the human body every minute (bad news)
- Every day an adult body produces 300 billion new cells (good news)
- The human body contains roughly 37 trillion (37,000,000, 000,000) cells (mind-boggling news)
- DNA, the stranding of genetic code located in each human cell, tells the cell what to do—a sort of internal computer

within each cell. Each adult human body has six-and-a-half-foot lengths of DNA strand in each cell, and if all the strands in a human body could be strung together, it would stretch from earth to the sun and back—seventy times![8] Yes, I double-checked it.

Do you see? *You are a universe* . . . with your own galaxies of plans, interests, thoughts, feelings, systems, and movements. They are orbiting and swirling now—they always are—most often without a single consideration from you. And God ordained and sustains all of it.

His wisdom is a holy wisdom. It is unsearchable.

With Him are wisdom and might; To Him belong counsel and understanding.

Job 12:13

Do you not know? Have you not heard? The Everlasting God, the Lord, the Creator of the ends of the earth does not become weary or tired. His understanding is inscrutable.

Isaiah 40:28

Not only this, but think about how the world would be different if *you* had made it. Would you have ever thought to procreate human life from an experience so amazing as sex? A treasured blessing to a husband and wife and family, and simultaneously a built-in education in responsibility for all those who would abuse its power?

Would you have ever thought of giraffes or jazz music?

Would you have ever thought of love? That the way to make yourself most happy is choosing to make yourself less happy in order to make someone else more happy . . . having both people been made happier through the process?

Would you have ever thought of Einstein or Wayne Gretzky or Hitler?

Would you have thought of greatness through service? That

the way to be a great leader is not to seek power but to give it to others?

Or what about this? We talked about the intricacy of the human body. What about the sheer vastness of the web of human thought and imagination? What about the networks of human knowledge and how they intertwine to display the glory and wisdom of God? Take science as one small example. Science owes a debt to mathematics to process information. It owes a debt to history to apprehend what's happened in the past. It owes a debt to language to communicate ideas. It owes a debt to philosophy and religion to understand beginnings. It owes a debt to the arts to give constant reminder of the world's wonder and value.

Every discipline of knowledge in God's world exists with unlimited, untapped potential. We are forever mining the caves—exploring, discovering, unfolding the manifold wisdom of God. We were designed to resign ourselves to Someone much smarter than us.

> "For My thoughts are not your thoughts, nor are your ways My ways," declares the Lord. "For as the heavens are higher than the earth, so are My ways higher than your ways, and My thoughts than your thoughts."
>
> Isaiah 55:8–9

The Glory of God's Sovereignty

God's rule presides over every mega-star and every human cell.

As R.C. Sproul says, there is not one maverick molecule in the universe. Since all things are "from Him" and are sustained "through Him," all things owe a debt of allegiance "to Him" (Romans 11:36).[9]

That which God makes God owns.

As Abraham Kuyper famously said, "There is not a square inch in the whole domain of our human existence over which Christ, who is Sovereign over all, does not cry, Mine!"[10]

Amen. God reigns.

Most would give a hearty "Amen" to that.

The problem comes (for me included) when we see that God's reigning, according to the Bible, is not merely an overarching general control. Rather, *God plans and determines every single thing that happens in His universe.*

I should repeat that.

God plans and determines every single thing that happens in His universe.

Like a composer strategically places every single note for every single measure for every single instrument for its exact designated duration.

Not a meteor, molecule, or mouth moves without God's command.

He is sovereign. Amen. God reigns.

Amen?

(Crickets)

The sovereignty of God is the happy, unchallenged, free exercise of His will. It is: God does what God wants. Period.

This doctrine is difficult.

Its glory makes us squint, but I hope you'll look with me.

Charles Spurgeon said it this way, "I believe that every particle of dust that dances in the sunbeam does not move an atom more or less than God wishes."[11]

Every particle of dust? Have you considered this before? Well, consider it again. God's sovereignty is a matchless sovereignty.

We've heard enough from the dead guys. Let's hear now what God says about God's sovereignty.

Since sovereignty is somewhat of a combination of power and wisdom, which we have already peered into, I am simply going to point you to some relevant Scriptures.

Sit with them. Read them. Pray them. Write about them if you want.

Celebrate the One they describe.

God Is Sovereign Over All Things

Worthy are You, our Lord and our God, to receive glory and honor and power; for You created all things, and because of Your will they existed, and were created."

Revelation 4:11

For by Him all things were created, both in the heavens and on earth, visible and invisible, whether thrones or dominions or rulers or authorities—all things have been created through Him and for Him. He is before all things, and in Him all things hold together.

Colossians 1:16–17

God Is Sovereign Over All Human Life

The mind of man plans his way,
But the Lord directs his steps.

Proverbs 16:9

Thus says God the Lord,
Who created the heavens and stretched them out,
Who spread out the earth and its offspring,
Who gives breath to the people on it
And spirit to those who walk in it.

Isaiah 42:5

God Is Sovereign Over the Womb

Abraham prayed to God, and God healed Abimelech and his wife and his maids, so that they bore children. For the Lord had closed fast all the wombs of the household of Abimelech because of Sarah, Abraham's wife.

Genesis 20:17–18

Is anything too difficult for the Lord? At the appointed time I will return to you, at this time next year, and Sarah will have a son.

Genesis 18:14

God Is Sovereign Over All Nature

And the Lord appointed a great fish to swallow Jonah, and Jonah was in the stomach of the fish three days and three nights.

Jonah 1:17

So the Lord God appointed a plant and it grew up over Jonah to be a shade over his head to deliver him from his discomfort. And Jonah was extremely happy about the plant. But God appointed a worm when dawn came the next day and it attacked the plant and it withered.

Jonah 4:6–7

Look at the birds of the air, that they do not sow, nor reap nor gather into barns, and yet your heavenly Father feeds them. Are you not worth much more than they?

Matthew 6:26

God Is Sovereign Over All Weather

He causes the vapors to ascend from the ends of the
earth;
Who makes lightnings for the rain,
Who brings forth the wind from His treasuries.

Psalm 135:7

And He got up and rebuked the wind and said to the sea, "Hush, be still." And the wind died down and it became perfectly calm.

Mark 4:39

God Is Sovereign Over All Kings and Kingdoms

It is He who changes the times and the epochs;
He removes kings and establishes kings;
He gives wisdom to wise men
And knowledge to men of understanding.

Daniel 2:21

The king's heart is like channels of water in the hand of
the Lord;
He turns it wherever He wishes.

Proverbs 21:1

God Is Sovereign Over All Evil, Pain, and Suffering

See now that I, I am He,
And there is no god besides Me;
It is I who put to death and give life.
I have wounded and it is I who heal,
And there is no one who can deliver from My hand.

Deuteronomy 32:39

He said, "Naked I came from my mother's womb,
And naked I shall return there.
The Lord gave and the Lord has taken away.
Blessed be the name of the Lord."

Job 1:21

The Lord kills and makes alive;
He brings down to Sheol and raises up.
The Lord makes poor and rich;
He brings low, He also exalts.

1 Samuel 2:6–7

God Is Sovereign Over Salvation

No one has taken it away from Me, but I lay it down on My
own initiative. I have authority to lay it down, and I have authority to take it up again. This commandment I received from
My Father.

John 10:18

For by grace you have been saved through faith; and that not
of yourselves, it is the gift of God; not as a result of works, so
that no one may boast.

Ephesians 2:8–9

You did not choose Me but I chose you, and appointed you that you would go and bear fruit, and that your fruit would remain, so that whatever you ask of the Father in My name He may give to you.

John 15:16

God Is Sovereign Over All Seemingly Random Details

Are not two sparrows sold for a cent? And yet not one of them will fall to the ground apart from your Father. But the very hairs of your head are all numbered.

Matthew 10:29–30

Come now, you who say, "Today or tomorrow we will go to such and such a city, and spend a year there and engage in business and make a profit." Yet you do not know what your life will be like tomorrow. You are just a vapor that appears for a little while and then vanishes away. Instead, you ought to say, "If the Lord wills, we will live and also do this or that."

James 4:13–15

The Glory We See

The interesting thing about the attributes of God we have examined in this chapter is that nearly all of them can be deduced from the world around us and from philosophy.

The Bible says it this way: "For since the creation of the world *His invisible attributes, His eternal power and divine nature, have been clearly seen, being understood* through what has been made, so that they are without excuse" (Romans 1:20).

At the risk of sounding insensitive, I'll go ahead and say what this verse means: There is no such thing as an atheist.

If you are an atheist, please know I don't think you are stupid. I don't think you are more of a sinner than I am. I don't even think that you don't have any good reasons to believe what you do, because you do.

I'm just saying . . . that based on this verse . . . that deep down . . . maybe way deep down . . . you know God exists. We all do.

My problem is the same as yours: *I don't want Him to exist.*

Most of the atheists I know or have met have been deeply angry about something that happened to them. I always want to ask, "Why are you so mad"?

When we are angry, we are appealing to a sense of fairness or justice that was violated. Why do we do this?

Because deep down we know there is a God who is Just.

Even if we "preach" that life is meaningless, we simply can't live that way. We can't. You want to (need to) be treated better than a random blob of molecules, and so do I.

By a thoughtful look inside us and around us, we can make a lot of meaningful conclusions.

Because of cause and effect, we can conclude that "Nothing + No One = Everything" probably doesn't work.

Because of thermodynamics and expended energy, we can say that the universe is probably not eternal.

We can look at the blazing stars, the mountain ranges, the untamed oceans, and the bizarre animals and know that there must be Someone who did all this, and if He did, He would be eternal. He would be powerful. He would be wise. He would be sovereign.

This is exactly what Romans 1 is telling us: " . . . because that which is known about God is evident *within them;* for God made it *evident to them"* (v. 19).

Whether we look within us or without us, we know there is a God and we know "that which is known" about Him. Augustine echoed Romans 1 in his own brilliant way so many years ago:

"And what is God?" I asked the earth, and it answered, "I am not He;" and everything in the earth made the same confession. I asked the sea and the deeps and the creeping things, and they replied, "We are not your God; seek above us." I asked the fleeting winds, and the whole air with its inhabitants answered, "Anaximenes was deceived; I am not God." I asked the heavens, the sun, moon, and stars; and they answered, "Neither are we the God whom you seek." And I replied to all these things which stand around the door of my flesh: "You have told me about my God, that you are not He. Tell me something about Him." And with a loud voice they all cried out, "He made us." My question had come from my observation of them, and their reply came from their beauty of order. And I turned my thoughts into myself and said, "Who are you?" And I answered, "A man. . . ." I asked the whole frame of earth about my God, and it answered, "I am not He, but He made me."

Augustine's Confessions, Book 10

We have all seen and heard, but as Romans 1:18 tells us, we have suppressed the truth in unrighteousness.

We don't suppress something accidentally. We suppress something if we see a real problem threatening a false image we have made—a truth we need to suffocate under a lie. That is what we have done with the glory of God.

For even though they knew God, they did not honor Him as God or give thanks, but they became futile in their speculations, and their foolish heart was darkened. Professing to be wise, they became fools, *and exchanged the glory of the incorruptible God for an image in the form of corruptible man and of birds and four-footed animals and crawling creatures.*

Romans 1:21–23

We have all seen glory, and exchanged it. Betrayed it. We have all seen the same dazzling sliver of His excellence, and sadly, we have misaimed.

3

Bad Aim
(Glory and Sin)

When we cease to worship God, we do not worship nothing.
We worship anything.

G. K. Chesterton

God at the brothel door
We're all seeking something more
All seeking something more
What are you looking for
Staring at the brothel door
You were made for so much more

"At the Brothel Door"
from the *Look & Live* album

The year was 336 BC. Ancient Macedonia's king had fallen
to an assassin. Now his noble son, Alexander the Great,
took the throne. A student of Aristotle, he had a spark of ambition in his eye that could ignite a frozen tundra. (At least that

is what people said. And I thought only superheroes could do this sort of thing.)

He started with Thessaly. He overpowered the Thracians, crushed the Illyrians, and then he moved on to Thebes.

Check.

Next was Persia and Tyre. Check.

Then he hit a slow year and was only able to conquer Gaza, Egypt, and Babylon. (Hey, if you've got "The Great" next to your name, the expectations are high.)

After conquering most of the known world (all the Mediterranean from Egypt to India), he made his final conquest to Punjab, but by this time, his men were so exhausted they all went home.

So Alexander the Great, now largely alone, decided he would spend some time and take inventory of all his success. He gathered his advisors, entered his tent, sat down, and there . . .

He wept.

From joy? No. *From despair.*

It seems Alexander the Great didn't really have it all. In truth, what he had was a God-void.

We have one, too.

We are trying to find the Embrace. Our true Home. The real Glory. The Infinitely Interesting.

And so we search for it in stuff, in approval from people, in pornography, in gaining power. But this replacing process, of course, doesn't ever work.

Ask Alexander. Ask yourself.

An idol, simply put, is anything that is more important to you than God. It is anything that has outweighed God in your life—anything that you love, trust, or obey more than God—anything that has replaced God as essential to your happiness.

God is missing from the human heart, and we are all now, as J. R. R. Tolkien famously said, "soaked with the sense of exile."[1]

But it has not always been this way.

The Door to Idolatry

Once upon a time, in a land not so far away, lived a certain man and a certain woman. Certain, they were, of the most incredible truth in the world: that they were held in the highest regard by the highest Being.

God loved them, and they knew it. Really knew it.

Because of this certainty, they needed nothing. Nothing but Him.

Sure, they loved and enjoyed the world. They actually enjoyed it more than we do. But that's because they didn't enjoy it as an end in itself. They loved the One who made it more, and this made everything, in a real sense, right.

But things quickly went wrong.

This man and this woman had an enemy who wanted to decisively break their unbreakable joy, to interrupt their uninterruptible peace.

"God's holding out on you two. His presence is great, I'm sure, but don't you want real happiness?"

> The serpent said to the woman, "You surely will not die! For God knows that in the day you eat from [the tree], your eyes will be opened, and you will be like God, knowing good and evil."
>
> Genesis 3:4–5

He offered them knowledge. Power. Glory. A "the Great" beside each of their names. He offered them something more than God.

Funny how that always turns out to be . . .

Less.

Idolatry.

They bit the apple hook, and were reeled in.

Now on a shore of emptiness, loneliness, nakedness.

Here they were. Here we are.

Made for the ocean, but now searching.

Wandering. Restless. God-less.

Nothing would ever be, has ever been, the same.

We have taken the diamond of God's glory to the pawn shop of the world and traded it for a penny.

A Diamond for a picture of a diamond.

That's the greatest injustice in the universe. That's idolatry.

Idolatry is essentially misaimed worship. Consider the fundamental relationship between misdirected worship and sin from a famous verse from the book of Romans: "For all have sinned and fall short of the glory of God" (3:23).

Most of the time, when this verse is considered, we place the emphasis on the word *all* to demonstrate the verse's haunting pervasiveness.

All have sinned. That's everyone. Me. You.

Yes, it's true. There's no denying it.

The question that many like to ask is, What about the innocent man in Africa who's never heard the name of Jesus?

"Can he be saved?" is a faulty question on its surface. There is no such thing as an innocent man in Africa, or anywhere else.

Back to Romans 3:23.

Let's hone in on the word *sinned*. In the Greek, the word *sinned* is *hamartia*, which means "to miss the mark," an archery term.

Maybe you've heard this before?

I had heard it my whole life growing up around church, but it never meant much to me until I connected the archery metaphor to worship.

Think about it.

What is the "target" in this verse?

The target is "the glory of God"—the thing we were made to contemplate, admire, and enjoy. For all have sinned and fall short of the glory of God.

But what about the arrows? What are they?

Worship.

The arrows are the deepest affections and longings of my soul, which are continually being aimed and fired toward *something*.

Some glory.

Like an automatic weapon, worship is happening. Now. As you read this.

We are all always squinting our eyes and zeroing in on *something*. And that something was always meant to be the excellency and infinite worth of God.

But we have aimed poorly. I have aimed poorly.

All have sinned. And fall short.

We, like Alexander, have sought to conquer kingdoms—to build our names, our dreams, our comforts—and in doing so we have not sought too much but too little. We have not aimed too high but far, far too low.

Bad Aim—Why?

So what are we looking at? Aiming at?

As mentioned earlier, an idol can be anything.

It could be money, sex, sports, a relationship. Even something like ministry can be an idol.

But most often, these things are not the ultimate target.

Tim Keller, in his book *Counterfeit Gods*,[2] gives some very helpful categories for idolatry: "surface idols" and "root idols."

Surface idols are things like social media or your smartphone. They can be anything.

But root idols are those deeper desires of the human heart that are generally in three categories: (1) fame and approval; (2) power and control; and (3) comfort and security. They are the reasons we can't stop checking our social media. And we find these desires—these restless waves—surging at the root of all sin.

Let's look.

In Exodus 20, God is giving his household the family rules— rules that He tells His kids will make life work best, also known as the Ten Commandments.

The first command is, "I am the Lord your God, who brought you out of the land of Egypt, out of the house of slavery. You shall have no other gods before Me" (v. 1–2).

#1. Most important. Pay attention!

God says, No idols!

Then he goes on to repeat himself nine times.

How so?

Well, consider commandment #4: "Remember the Sabbath day" (v. 8). Or, put positively: Live a life of ordered, balanced rest.

Now, not many of us do this well, especially in our modern, fast-paced culture. *Rest is for the weak . . . for the faint of heart,* we think. *There's work to be done, for goodness sake.*

Why are we like this? Why can't we seem to slow down? Why are we enslaved to our work? Why do we break this commandment?

I'll tell you why I break it.

It's not because I worship work or money. It's much deeper. I want applause. I need applause. I want power and fame, and I'll hurt myself or my family to get it.

Now consider commandment #6: "You shall not murder" (v. 13).

Jesus tells us in the New Testament that if you look on another person with hatred in your heart, you have committed murder. So why are we bitter? Why can't we forgive others? Why do we break this commandment?

I'll tell you why I break it.

I get angry at others when they threaten my idols. When someone gets in the way of my time, my career, my applause, my comfort, what I want, I "murder" them. I strip them of their dignity to preserve my own, only to find that my dignity has committed suicide.

Lastly, let's consider commandment #9: "You shall not bear false witness against your neighbor" (v. 16). In other words, do not lie.

Why do we grossly exaggerate stories? Why do we cheat the numbers? Why do we break this commandment?

I'll tell you why I break it.

I lie when I want to make myself look better. I like to get approval. I remember just the other day I was traveling somewhere, and a local asked me if I had been to his part of the world before. My response was, "I don't know . . . I think so." But I knew I hadn't been there before. I just wanted to look well-traveled.

Ridiculous idolatry.

I wanted approval and power in that moment more than I wanted God.

Disordered Loves Make Disordered Lives

An idol is typically a good thing that has become a god-thing.

Augustine called idolatry "disordered love."

It is when we love something more than God that we unleash chaos in our lives.

If you want to find your idols, trace your most unyielding emotions. Anger, despair, anxiety . . . What are they coming from? These emotions are like smoke from the fire of the altar of the god that you're worshiping.

And the tricky thing is, emotions are not necessarily bad, so it makes the idols hard to find sometimes. They can hide themselves. Sometimes for a long time.

Recently my wife and I were talking about her "sin issues." (I got permission from my wife to share this.) She was telling me that she was having the hardest time with anxiety and anger around the house.

The house always felt like a wreck, and when she would try to clean a room, the kids would always want to "help" her. Then the girls would get in an argument. More chaos. Then Lauren would snap at them and feel bad about it.

After talking about it, it became somewhat apparent that power and control tends to be a root idol for my wife. The funny thing is, she had never even thought about it, never even noticed it.

What a root idol can do is hide itself. Occasionally it will manifest itself in sinful ways.

Our emotions flare up when our god gets threatened—when there is an obstacle between us and what we truly love.

Now, I am by no means downplaying the chaos that a mom endures on a daily basis. I am not saying that all frustration stems from idolatry. But unyielding frustration most definitely does.

Peace in your home is a good thing. But my wife has found that when the arrows of her worship are aimed at circumstantial peace, she never can lay hold of supernatural peace (which God gives), which is really what she's after anyway.

Speaking of peace in our house . . .

We have three daughters, ages five, three, and one, who love to have dance parties. Almost every night after dinner we kick up the music and flail our bodies in total abandon.

My wife and I can sometimes be a little bashful, but our daughters know nothing of this so-called self-awareness. They just go for it. Sometimes they get so into it that they start throwing off their clothes! That's how we know that the dance party was a success . . . if we end up with three precious, panting, naked little girls in the living room.

The fascinating thing to me is that Paisley and Stella love to be naked. Most all little kids do. They really don't know what clothes are for, and the reason is because they don't know what nakedness is. There is not an ounce of shame or embarrassment in their eyes. Only joy. Why? Because they are with Mom and Dad, and they know they are totally safe and totally loved.

Before there was sin, there were two grown-ups in a garden buck naked. Exposed. Unprotected. Undisguised. Unashamed.

They had no clothes because they were already clothed in the love of God. But they decided to play with fire. They stepped outside God's loving boundaries and then did one of the saddest things in all the Bible, in all the world.

They hid from God.

I cry as I write this. They had always been naked, but now they *felt naked*. They let doubt creep in, and now they weren't sure anymore if God loved them. And so our grasping for fig leaves began.

My three sinners—ahem, I mean *daughters*—I love them dearly, but it's true, they are idolaters just like their dad. Sometimes my oldest, Paisley, will misplace her worship onto her blocks, and when she does, she likes to prevent my middle daughter, Stella, from enjoying them.

"Mine!" Paisley snarls as she gathers the blocks to herself like they are hundred-dollar bills. She throws her little body around the blocks and begins nervously peering and panting toward her sister to make sure she doesn't snag one. Then Stella starts crying. And the irony is, you would think Paisley would be happy now, right? She has what she wants. But it seems that her mission has been a self-defeating one. She's not happy. She's just anxious, tired, and alone.

Are we that much different? Are we more mature? No. We don't mature. Our idols do. And it's not blocks anymore. It's our free time. Our wallet. Our sport. Our degree. Our car. Our dignity. We're older now, but at the end of the day, we're just little kids who have their lives wrapped around something that isn't God, screaming "Mine!" and hurting anyone who gets in the way of what we want.

What are we doing when we make our career an idol?

Why, we're just covering up. We aren't totally sure anymore that God loves us, so we climb the ladder and push people down on our way up.

Fig leaf.

What are we doing when we make our appearance an idol?

Reaching to a fig branch.

If we knew that we were held in the highest regard by the

highest Being, we wouldn't care what we looked like. But we have forgotten this.

There is a veil over our heart's eyes.

And so we envy those who are good-looking and feel superior to those who aren't. We blow money on our appearance.

We are professional fig-leaf collectors.

We anxiously search for better fig leaves.

We flaunt our designer fig leaves. But at the end of the day, they're just fig leaves, and we're still anxious, alone, and tired.

Idolatry breeds anxiety because deep down, way deep down, we know that the thing we are clinging to is not permanent.

Have you ever thought about why God commands us to love Him with all our heart, soul, mind, and strength?

Is it because God is an egomaniac?

Because He's needy? Lonely?

No.

God is a good daddy, and good daddys don't give their kids commands for no reason. They don't give their kids commands in order to earn more power or handcuff their kids' happiness.

God commands us to love Him more than anything else because He knows that anything we love more than Him is going to betray us.

The Blasphemy of Idolatry

The worst part of idolatry is not the despair it leads to.

It's not the relational chaos it unleashes. It's not the anxiety that it necessitates or the devastation it leads to in our lives.

The worst part of idolatry is that we have offended God. Despised and rejected God.

There are great injustices in the world today. Children dying of starvation, women trafficked as sex slaves, infants brutally murdered in the womb . . . These are terrible things.

But there is no greater injustice than this—that God is not worshiped.

Take a moment to let that sink in, because, like coming out of a dark room into the light, it is something our eyes have to adjust to.

Because starvation, slavery, and murder are tangible, physical things we can see, we automatically elevate them as supreme because they are immediate to our lives. We have to "squint" for a while to remember that He is the *most* precious Being in the universe, and we have set him aside. Even we Christians have.

We have used God. Like a bride who says "I do" and then ditches the guy for his money, we have married God for His money.

We have made Him a means to an end.

This is the greatest or paramount injustice, and all others stem from this.

Psalm 51 illustrates this blasphemy for us. This psalm is David's famous prayer of confession after he murdered a man and slept with his wife.

Did you hear me?

Murdered a man and slept with his wife. This is "varsity" sinning. These are grave injustices. But look how David prays:

> Have mercy on me, O God, according to your unfailing love; according to your great compassion blot out my transgressions. . . . *Against you, you only, have I sinned and done what is evil in your sight.*
>
> Psalm 51:1, 4 NIV

Against "You" only? Against God only?

Hey, David, what about against Uriah or Bathsheba?!? Did you forget about them?

Yes, I actually think he did. Because at that moment, David was in the presence of the One who breathed galaxies into being. He was in the presence of the Holy. And in the light of that blinding Goodness, David saw his own smallness and his sin's blackness. He realized his sin against God was so great, it was as if he had sinned against no one else.

If I disrespect my parents, the person most offended is God.

If I turn my back on the poor, the person most offended is God.

If I cheat on my wife, the person most offended is God.

Let's take this a little further. Believe it or not, one of the places that we most clearly see the beauty and worth of God is hell. Hell?

Yes.

The doctrine of hell is obviously an offensive doctrine. It has been for centuries, and certainly is today in our culture of relativism and non-judgmentalism. But it is not only offensive as an idea, it is also personally offensive.

When we talk about hell, we are not just talking about concepts, we're talking about people. Real people under the eternal, righteous judgment of God.

So I do not want to speak about it lightly. I'm not trying to win an argument here. The doctrine of hell is a polarizing doctrine. It will lead you to run or to worship. I'm praying for the latter.

In God's world, every evil action demands a consequence.

If I got angry at my pastor one day and decided to punch him in the face (let's just say I was having a bad day), the consequence would perhaps be the loss of his friendship, my job, or probably both. If things got really violent and he decided to call the cops, and I punched the cop in the face, my consequence would probably be jail. Then let's say things escalated and I got sent to the state capitol building, and I punched the governor in the face. Then I get sent to the Supreme Court, and . . . well, you get the point. What would happen to me then?

In this metaphor, the sin was always the same: a punch in the face. However, the "sinned against" was different, and consequences for sin always increase with the degree of the authority of the offended. What makes sin so evil, so damnable, is not the ugliness of the act itself but Who the act is against.

We have defied God.

Some might say, "Sure, I confess I've done some bad things, but I haven't been nearly as bad as some people. I mean, come on, what about Hitler?"

My reply?

Judging holiness by the standard of other men is useless. Two men standing at the foot of Mt. Everest don't argue about who is taller. They look up and tremble.

The Eternity of Idolatry

Many times people have a view of hell that is a far cry from reality. It usually goes something like this. . . .

I die, and then I get taken up before God, who is sitting on a lofty, white throne with some fog around it. There's a gate to heaven on my left and a gate to hell on my right. I fall down on my knees as He asks me, "Why should I let you into my heaven?"

I begin to make my case.

Midway, God motions to His angels who come and grab me by the arms and start to drag me off to hell. I begin screaming, "No, please, God! I want to go to heaven! Please! Have mercy!"

But there is no mercy. It's too late.

And I am pushed through the gate. Against my will.

C. S. Lewis taught a much different view of hell (and a more biblical one, I believe). According to the Bible and Lewis, hell is not a place that we are thrown into, it is a place that we *grow* into. It is what we become, what we want. We really don't love God or worship God, and therefore, like Lucifer, we would rather have our idols than be truly happy.

It's only logical.

If we did not spend any time on earth worshiping God, why would we want to spend all eternity doing that?

If we didn't spend any time on earth fellowshiping with other believers, why would we want to do that forever?

Hell is merely the continuation of earthly rebellion. Hell is eternal idolatry.

Idolatry means misery. It is the source of all disorder, despair, disappointment, destruction, and ultimately death. When we try to make a heaven of earth, we unleash hell on earth. Tim Keller said it well: "Hell is just your freely chosen identity, based on something else besides God, going on forever."[3]

Lewis, in *The Great Divorce*, explained it this way:

> "Milton was right," said my Teacher. "The choice of every lost soul can be expressed in the words 'Better to reign in Hell than serve in Heaven.' There is always something they insist on keeping, even at the price of misery. There is always something they prefer to joy—that is, to reality. We see it easily enough in a spoiled child that would sooner miss its play and its supper than say it was sorry and be friends. . . .There are only two kinds of people in the end: those who say to God, 'Thy will be done,' and those to whom God says, in the end, 'Thy will be done.'"[4]

Stop Sinning! (How to Change)

Maybe by this point, you're saying, "Thanks a lot, Matt. You've written a book that reminds me of what I already knew too well: The world's a mess, and so am I."

Okay. So let's get to it then.

How do we change? How do we get unstuck? Un-addicted? How do we become people who worship God and not our idols?

Here's how: You do better. You do more.

I've heard it my whole life. You get busy. Religious. You try harder. You get accountability. You hunker down and finally do it. You actually check off everything on the checklist.

No!

We worship our way into sin, so again, we must worship our way out.

In the early 1800s, a pastor named Thomas Chalmers preached a famous sermon entitled "The Expulsive Power of a New Affection," in which he made the revolutionary claim that we don't ultimately, or fundamentally, change by trying harder but rather by seeing Glory.

He said that since we cannot *not* worship—since the heart is a throne that must be occupied—we don't change simply by removing what's there. We don't change by saying, "Bad soul! Stop worshiping that."

We cannot keep continually dragging our idols off the throne. That throne is a magnet, and this process is utterly exhausting and otherwise known as religion.

No willpower, sheer human grit, or determination will overthrow that pseudo god. It will not be removed; in fact, it cannot be. Idols are never removed. They are replaced. Displaced. They are not suppressed. They are eclipsed.

Jonathan Edwards (essentially) said it this way: We always do what we most desire to do.[5]

You might say, "No way, that's not true. I don't enjoy waking up and going to school or work every morning."

Oh, but you do. You enjoy making money and living comfortably more than you enjoy a little extra sleep. And so you go off to work. You always do what you most desire to do.

We are desire-driven creatures, and will always desire, enjoy, and act upon our highest perceived good.

Blaise Pascal said it this way: "We forsake pleasures only for others which are greater."[6]

How does the boy who is hopelessly addicted to video games break his childish habit? Well, how else? He finds a greater pleasure. He becomes addicted to making money—to career, you might say—a more "mature" idol, as mentioned earlier. He sees a greater glory. His idol is replaced.

All men seek happiness. This is without exception. Whatever different means they employ, they all tend to this end. The cause of some going to war, and of others avoiding it, is the same desire in both, attended with different views. The will never takes the least step but to this object. This is the motive of every action of every man, even of those who hang themselves.[7]

Blaise Pascal

In 2 Corinthians 3, Paul is talking about Moses and the Ten Commandments and how they came in glory:

> But if the ministry of death, in letters engraved on stones, came with glory, so that the sons of Israel could not look intently at the face of Moses because of the glory of his face, fading as it was, how will the ministry of the Spirit fail to be even more with glory? For if the ministry of condemnation has glory, much more does the ministry of righteousness abound in glory. *For indeed what had glory, in this case has no glory because of the glory that surpasses it.*

2 Corinthians 3:7–10

There it is. Glory-surpassing glory.

Then there's Matthew 13:44, the man with the treasure in the field. Why did he sell *everything*? Why did he get all "radical"? Because he felt obligated? Because some red-faced preacher told him to? No. He did it because when he looked at the field, he didn't see a bunch of dirt and grass. He saw a treasure.

And here again:

> But we all, with unveiled face, *beholding as in a mirror the glory of the Lord, are being transformed* into the same image from glory to glory, just as from the Lord, the Spirit.

2 Corinthians 3:18

How does this verse tell us we are transformed? By having perfect church attendance? By gritting our teeth and doing better? Tithing 11 percent? Trying harder? No.

We are changed when we see glory-within. We are transformed when we see the radiance of God.

I could never seem to shake the porn addiction. I had the accountability, the computer software, everything but real victory. As much as I wanted to stop, I couldn't. The idol just seemed to jump right back on the throne. But then I got some advice from a mentor friend of mine.

He said to me, "Matt, I know you've been fighting, but have you been *looking?*"

Huh?

What he meant was had I really been spending time with Jesus? In the hustle and bustle of life, I hadn't.

And so I did. I really did.

I began just soaking in the Bible every morning. I woke up and just looked at Jesus. And it didn't happen overnight, but slowly, something began happening. I started tasting freedom. I began changing.

I met Glory.

That's how we change, by experiencing a greater Thrill.

Sadly, much of Christian teaching today will tell us to change using one of two strategies, both of which are powerless.

The first is what we call *religion*. This is the do better, try harder, idol-removing approach. In that same "Expulsive Power" sermon mentioned earlier, Thomas Chalmers compared this to a preacher telling a man with a mansion to burn down his mansion because that is a more "Christian way" to live. Powerless. There is no positive reason for the man to do so. If, however, the preacher said, "There is a bigger mansion waiting for you if you will just burn down your current shack," the man would be running to get his blowtorch.

Why?

Glory-surpassing glory. That's how desires change. That's how people change.

The other approach is what we will call *secularism*. This approach compels people to change by essentially using "idol-swapping" techniques.

"Your life will go better if you give up this habit."

"Believe in yourself."

"God takes care of those who take care of themselves."

"If you give Jesus 10 percent, you'll be wealthy."

While some of these statements have the hint of truth in them, none of them are rooted in the glory of God, and therefore, they are powerless. They amount to the example of the boy giving up his video-game addiction for a more mature addiction, namely career.

Idols replacing other idols, breaking the heart of their worshiper. An endless cycle of despair.

Real Christianity shows us a glory so great that it effortlessly eclipses all other would-be glories, and a God so ineffable that He can forever satisfy us, enthrall us, and ultimately, change us.

Yet, we have seen His glory in creation but have not responded in worship. Is this God's fault? Is His glory not great enough?

No.

Our foolish hearts have been darkened (Romans 1:21) and the god of this world has blinded the minds of the unbelieving (2 Corinthians 4:4). The eyes of our heart are now covered by a veil of doubt (2 Corinthians 3:15).

So how will the veil be removed? How will we change?

How else?

A bigger target.

A greater Glory.

4

The Blazing Center

The apex of the glory of God is the grace of God, and the apex
of the grace of God is the slaughter of the Lamb of God.

John Piper

My eyes have seen the beauty of the cross
Where holiness and infinite mercy shine
I cannot dream of something more than this
So Father take me deeper into its light

Pull back the veil and leave my idols crucified
This flesh is frail but this is why I live

I'm praying . . .

"Show Me Your Glory"
from the *Look & Live* album

The day we met, I was captivated.

After our five-minute conversation, I called the guys in
my band and told them I had just met my wife.

In that precious five minutes, though, I found out that in five months she was heading overseas to be a missionary. A cute little missionary. She was going for four years.

Four years?!?

I had to work fast.

Now, in any budding guy/girl relationship, there's a line that exists—a line between "pursuing" and "stalking." And I was toeing that bad boy the whole time.

(Okay, so maybe I crossed it a couple of times.)

I called the church where I met her. "Hey, um, so there's this girl named Lauren who goes to your church. She's cute, short brown hair . . . heading to do overseas missions."

A long pause. "Yeah? And?"

"Well, I was, um . . . just wondering if I could get her phone number?"

"Um. Sir, that's awkward."

"I know, I know, I know, I'm sorry," I said. Eventually, after talking to a few people, the youth pastor knew me well enough that he gave me her phone number.

I called her up and we met for a romantic lunch at the IHOP to "talk about her mission trip."

I told Lauren that I would like to pursue her.

She said, "No, thanks."

I told her I was going to anyway.

She said, "Okay . . . ?"

A couple of weeks later, on Valentine's Day, I showed up with flowers at the restaurant where she worked. (She had never told me where she worked.)

I was in love.

She was confused (and probably a little nervous).

Over the next couple of months, Lauren and I really did have a great time together—all except for the awkward conversations I would impose upon her.

Twice more I told her that I was going to pursue her, and twice more she told me, "No, Matt! I'm leaving the country!"

Finally, I couldn't take the defeat any longer, and so I did what all intelligent guys do: I gave her an ultimatum. "I need you to either tell me this is going somewhere, or tell me, 'Matt, give up.'"

"Matt, give up."

I was crushed. That didn't pan out the way I had hoped. I shouldered the weight of those words, bowed my head, and respectfully gave Lauren her space.

But I didn't give up.

I refrained from texting, calling, or emailing for a month, which felt like an eternity when I knew my love was leaving soon.

Then I got a phone call about eight o'clock one night. When we finally said good-bye, it was eight in the morning.

I still hadn't given up, and I think something in Lauren knew that.

We started dating.

I proposed a couple of months later, and she said yes.

She moved overseas, came back eight months later, we said "I do," and the rest, as they say, is history.

My wife didn't fall in love with me because of my devilish good looks (that's a joke). She didn't fall in love with me because I swooped into her life one day and said, "Well, here I am. What are your other two wishes?" I didn't win her heart by flexing my muscles or showing her my résumé or commanding her to love me.

No, I pursued her. I made a fool of myself.

That's what won her heart. That's what she needed to see. A pursuit.

Where do we see the glory of God? The Bible says, "The heavens declare the glory of God" (Psalm 19:1 NIV). We see His glory all over creation. We see God "flexing His muscles" in the cosmos and displaying His intellect in the ten thousand unique species of ocean wildlife.

But despite all the glory all around us, all the beauty, something about it isn't enough. It's not enough to convince us, to arrest us, to melt the hardness of our doubting hearts. What we need to see is God "making a fool of himself."

What we need to see is a pursuit.

The Blazing Center (The Pursuit: Part 1)

Bethlehem. A humble town. A nobody's town. Perfect.

The mountains would have bowed down. The seas would have roared in praise. The trees clapped their hands. But not for this Ancient of Days. All He needed were a few shepherds and angels. And in this was His glory, not the towering greatness He laid aside, not His pomp or power or praise or pride, but His humility. His frailty. A little seven-pound, eight-ounce eternal weight of glory.

"Immensity cloistered in thy dear womb."[1]

Now He had come, full of grace and truth. "For unto us a child is born, unto us a son is given" (Isaiah 9:6 KJV). A child or Lord? This false division . . . a question rising throughout the ages, as mortal beings squint at greatness. Dawn of the ages. Incarnation.

And we beheld His glory. Veiled with infant body.

Selah.

The Glory of the Gospel

We are told in 2 Corinthians 3:18 that to behold "glory" is to change. But what is "glory" in this context? Is it some nebulous, cloudy light that we squint toward? Not really. In verse 14 Paul goes on to talk about how when the law is read, a veil lies over the hearts of the Jewish people. He says this veil is "removed in *Christ.*" In verse 16 he says "whenever a person *turns to the Lord*, the veil is taken away." Jump from verse 18 down into chapter 4 and we read these awesome words:

And even if our *gospel* is veiled, it is veiled to those who are perishing, in whose case the god of this world has blinded the minds of the unbelieving so that they might not see *the light of the gospel of the glory of Christ*, who is the image of God. For we do not preach ourselves but Christ Jesus as Lord, and ourselves as your bond-servants for Jesus' sake. For God, who said, "Light shall shine out of darkness," is the One who has shone in our hearts to give *the Light of the knowledge of the glory of God in the face of Christ*.

2 Corinthians 4:3–6

Paul is speaking about the gospel here. He's talking about salvation. He's talking about the blazing center—the cross. He's saying, "This is where you see glory! You see it in the pursuit. You see it in Jesus."

If you want to see some of God's glory, you can look at a sunset. But if you really want to see it, look at Jesus.

Jesus Christ is the image of the invisible God (Colossians 1:15). Jesus Christ is the radiance of the glory of God (Hebrews 1:3). He is the Word of God (John 1:1), the revelation of His *heart*.

What the universe, the heavens, could not reveal about God and His attributes, Jesus does . . . in spectacular, blinding array. In Jesus, we see the glory of God in stunning clarity and brilliance.

And this is the sweetest gift of the gospel.

Yes, through the gospel, we get our sins forgiven. Yes, we are set free from shame. Yes, we gain entrance into an eternal place where we never, ever suffer again. These things are staggering, but these things are not why the gospel is good news. They are not ultimate, but penultimate.

The gospel is good news because in the gospel we finally see a glory that will totally satisfy us and enthrall us forever—the glory of God.[2]

We are supposed to be stunned.

Our souls are supposed to be drinking with delight not merely gaining doctrinal clarity.

85

It is "the gospel of the glory of Christ" not "the glory of the gospel of Christ."

Gospel is the window.

Glory is the painting.

Salvation is the means.

Glory is the end.

But let me be clear: We must turn to Him. We must look to Him.

Seeing the glory of God in the face of Christ is a work of repentance.

The word *repentance*, because of its intimate association with salvation, once again points us to the Spirit and our dependence on Him. But it also tells us what is required of us.

> Whenever a person turns to the Lord, the veil is taken away.
>
> 2 Corinthians 3:16

The word *turns* there is *epistrepho*, which in the Greek means "to return." Paul's other usages of the word include Galatians 4:9 and 1 Thessalonians 1:9, which says, ". . . how you *turned* to God from idols to serve a living and true God." To truly look toward something is to repent of what you formerly looked toward. It is to consider the former thing not as satisfying or captivating.

This is Christian repentance. It is a turning away from the world and all of its pleasures toward Christ and all His superior pleasures.

It is a decisive, aggressive, blood-earnest looking.

In light of this, wherever you are in your faith journey, would you take some time now and just ask the Spirit to work in your heart—to lift the veil for you?

I want you to see Glory. That's why I wrote this book. Ask for His help, even if you have been a Christian for years.

The Blazing Center (The Pursuit: Part 2)

The years pass by, and now we see the Ancient One has grown.
He treads the ground that He spoke out those centuries before.

Authority.

This carpenter's son, He speaks not as one who wants power, but who has it.

Blind seeing, lame jumping, dead rising. . . . all things obeying the voice that made them.

In Him was life, and that life was the light of men.

But the darkness couldn't get it, comprehend it.

Religious elite, all blind to His brilliance. Masters of divinity, slaves to their ego. Trying to master Divinity, to tame Him, because they know—He's God.

He attracts and repels. With His band of twelve. Polarizing as hell.

"Eat my flesh, drink my blood."

Some bow. Some yell.

His signs and wonders, they're not for sale.

He's God.

But we all rebel.

Gazing at the Cross: Seeing Glory

We exist to contemplate and to celebrate the glory of God. Nothing else will be enough. But we could be more specific. We could say that we exist to contemplate and celebrate the *goodness* of God. Or, said another way, we were born to praise the glory of God's *grace.*

Earlier we discussed how the word *glory* can mean "value," "worth," or "goodness." In Exodus 33, when Moses prays, "Show me Your glory," God says, "I Myself will make all My *goodness* pass before you" (vv. 18–19). Therefore, the goodness of God, not some other aspect of Him, is the answer to Moses' prayer. Consider these words from a sermon on this very text by Charles Spurgeon:

> Now, what attribute is God about to show to Moses? His petition is, "Show me thy glory." Will he show him his justice?

Will he show him his holiness? Will he show his wrath? Will he show him his power? Will he break yon cedar and show him he is almighty? Will he rend yonder mountain and show him that he can be angry? Will he bring his sins to remembrance, and show that he is omniscient? No; hear the still small voice—"I will make all my goodness pass before thee." Ah! the goodness of God *is* God's glory. God's greatest glory is that he is good. The brightest gem in the crown of God is his goodness.[3]

In Ephesians 1, we learn that God made His rescue plan before the foundation of the world, not simply that we might glorify Him in general, but that we might glorify *His grace*.

> Blessed be the God and Father of our Lord Jesus Christ, who has blessed us with every spiritual blessing in the heavenly places in Christ, just as He chose us in Him before the foundation of the world, that we would be holy and blameless before Him. In love He predestined us to adoption as sons through Jesus Christ to Himself, according to the kind intention of His will, *to the praise of the glory of His grace*, which He freely bestowed on us in the Beloved.
>
> Ephesians 1:3–6

This passage says God blessed us, chose us, and predestined us "to the praise of the glory of His grace." The glorious work of salvation on the cross happened so that the goodness and grace of God might be praised specifically. Even His sovereign choice in salvation was designed to magnify His goodness: "What if God, although willing to demonstrate His wrath and to make His power known, endured with much patience vessels of wrath prepared for destruction? And He did so to make known the riches of His glory upon vessels of mercy, which He prepared beforehand for glory" (Romans 9:22–23).

This means that God's wrath is not some kind of counterbalance to His grace. It is the platform for it. God designed all of salvation—his choosing of some and not choosing others—to culminate in a rapturous, awe-filled celebration of the glory of *His goodness.*

Why does Jesus, after rising from the dead, still bear His scars? It can't be for no reason.

It has to be because God wanted every eternal sight of Him to be filled with the memory of His love.

In Revelation 5 we are told that this is exactly where all of history is heading. Time will culminate and all eternity will commemorate a Lamb that has been slaughtered, "who purchased . . . men for God from every tribe and tongue" (v. 9).

In Revelation 13 we are told that this was God's design—that before the dawn of time there was a book, and the book was called "the book of life of the Lamb who has been slain" (v. 8).

God designed the slaughter of His Son before the world so that His goodness might be eternally adored.

Throughout eternity, we will still be peering at the cross.

With awe, wonder, and surprise.

The Blazing Center (The Pursuit: Part 3)

Well, Glory knew His time had come.

A solemn dawn. A colder sun.

With holy furrowed brow, He knew somehow that this day was the moment.

Up on His feet, a face of flint, the race thus far was perfect.

But He must finish.

This weary God . . . weary from Almighty strain.

The miracles, the labor pains of passing on to mortal men eternal truth, they doubt again.

Patience.

The sleepless nights of fighting sin.

Face of flint.

But then, a smile begins. As He remembers.

Remembering as we remember. The joys of life.

The joys of friendship . . . of laughing with Peter . . . of cheering him on as he conquered water.

There was John the Baptist, who leapt in the womb—that untamed prophet: "Behold the Lamb!"

The dearest Marys and Lazarus, the smiling face of Zaccheus.

So many tears and joys to split, upon this world his fingerprints.

The joy was done.

And now the sprint.

For this He was meant.

Sent.

Lionhearted.

Face of flint.

Gazing at the Cross: Being Changed

One of the reasons I wrote this book was my love and respect for these words from Paul, which I'll share again:

> But we all, with unveiled face, beholding as in a mirror the glory of the Lord, are being transformed into the same image from glory to glory, just as from the Lord, the Spirit.
>
> 2 Corinthians 3:18

We change as we behold the glory of the Lord.

But notice *how* we change.

It doesn't say that when we see the glory of the Lord we want to change, although that is true. It doesn't say we begin desiring a changed life. It's more than that.

We "are being transformed."

On the spot. Changed. Right there.

That is the power of the gospel. That is the glory of God in the face of Christ. It is a thing so spectacular, so breathtaking, so wonderful, so powerful, that we are fundamentally rewired when we encounter it. We become something else.

And that is a theme scattered all over the Bible. Whenever human beings encounter God, they are not simply impacted, they are changed.

And the amazing thing is, none of them were *trying* to change. They just were changed.

When the Bible talks about salvation, it talks about being born again. No one tries to be born. It happens to you. The apostle John tells us in 1 John 3:1, "See how great a love the Father has bestowed on us, that we would be called children of God; and such we are." Such we are.

We become something else when we encounter the gospel.

Sometimes, when I ask people if they are a Christian, they respond with this answer: "I'm trying to be."

This articulates a misunderstanding of the religion. Christianity's first call is not "Behave!" but "Behold!" It is first a call to see Jesus.

Let's look at a few examples of this, starting with Zaccheus, the "wee little man."

Zaccheus was a tax collector, which means he was extremely wealthy and extremely disliked. The text says he was a "chief" tax collector, so he would have been unusually despicable. But Jesus saw him in that infamous sycamore and asked him to dinner with Him—a cordial sign of trust and companionship in that day. Jesus showed him grace. Jesus showed Zaccheus His glory. Let's look at what happened.

> Zaccheus stopped and said to the Lord, "Behold, Lord, half of my possessions I will give to the poor, and if I have defrauded anyone of anything, I will give back four times as much."
>
> Luke 19:8

Zaccheus is repenting, changing. He is being radical. Why? Is it because he was trying hard to be religious? To be piteous?

Quite the opposite. The word "behold" that is used there, in the original language, has the connotation of a child saying, "Look, Daddy!"

Zaccheus just wants Jesus to be proud of him. His heart is becoming mushy.

Let's ask another question: Was Zaccheus changed by seeing Jesus' power and sovereignty? Did he fall down in terror here over Jesus' wrath and justice?

Nope.

Smoke and mountains won't change us.

Only grace. Only a pursuit.

What about the woman caught in adultery, as described in John 8? We never find out her name, but this woman was caught by the scribes and Pharisees in the very act. There would have been so much shame, and rightfully so.

The religious had their stones ready.

Jesus . . . He was doing sand art.

"He who is without sin among you, let him be the first to throw a stone at her." Stones thud to sand. Then we read . . .

> Straightening up, Jesus said to her, "Woman, where are they? Did no one condemn you?" She said, "No one, Lord." And Jesus said, "I do not condemn you, either. Go. From now on sin no more."
>
> John 8:10–11

Why did this woman call Jesus "Lord"? Because of her goodness?

No, because of His.

Did she call Him "Lord" because Jesus flexed His God-muscles of power and might?

No, she called Him Lord because her life was in His hands, and He didn't crush her but caressed her. He showed her His glory.

And notice Jesus does not say here, "Go and sin no more, and I do not condemn you." It was "I do not condemn you, therefore, go and sin no more." The pronouncement is the power.

As Tim Keller says, "Only in the gospel do you get the verdict before the performance. I love you. Now love me. I love you. Now you *can* love me."[4]

Martyn Lloyd-Jones gives another wonderful example of the natural explosive power of the gospel to change us. Imagine a man who left several bills lying on his kitchen table. One day the man comes home from work and realizes his friend has paid off every debt.

How will the man respond to his friend?

Well, it probably depends on the value of the bills on the table.

If they totaled around fifty dollars, he might say, "Thanks, man!"

But if they were for twenty-five years of IRS tax evasion and added up $50,000, the man would probably fall to his knees and say, "Command me!"

This is the power of the gospel. This man did not struggle to surrender. He surrendered willingly when he saw the amount of his debt that had been paid.

When we see the penalty Jesus paid for us—the debt He absorbed into His own body—we will begin to surrender most naturally.

Many of us claim to have seen the cross, yet with our lives we are saying, "Thanks, man." We have not truly seen the cross until we say with every fiber of our being, "Command me! I am yours."

Consider the writings of the apostle Paul. Romans, Galatians, Ephesians, Philippians, and Colossians all begin the same way. With angry, red-faced pleading to obey God? With whip-cracking condemnation? No. Paul begins with theology. He says things like, "You are seated with Christ in the heavenly places," "God will complete His good work in you," "You were dead . . . now you are alive in Christ." And on and on and on. After that, once our eyes have been lifted up to God's glory, Paul moves on to practical living: "Husbands, love your wives," "Children, obey your parents," and so on. Why? Because that's the only order that works.

Paul does this in Romans perhaps most explicitly. He starts with eleven chapters of theology. Then comes a word that changes everything: *Therefore.*

> Therefore, I urge you, brethren, by the mercies of God, to present your bodies a living and holy sacrifice.
>
> Romans 12:1 NIV

Paul is not saying get out there and do better. No, he just put us on our backs with the most beautiful theology ever penned. He is saying you and I are different now. Now we have the power to obey.

Indicative then imperative. Glory then worship.

The Blazing Center (The Pursuit: Part 4)

A dinner planned. The Twelve convene.

The servant King knew the one who would betray Him, and yet he knelt and washed his reeking feet.

Royal and meek.

Bread broken. Wine passed. "Remember me."

Remember me. With not a hint of vain conceit. The mountains would have found their knees.

Remember me.

With passion and humility.

With solemnness, but underneath a joy that would have set a kingdom laughing.

Will set a kingdom laughing.

A man with a dream.

Remember me.

Where the Doubt Lives

My oldest daughter, Paisley, is at an age where she loves to ask "why." It seems to be her go-to response to everything I say.

"Paisley, please eat your broccoli."

"Why?"

"Paisley, don't stick your finger in the electrical outlet."

"Why?"

"Paisley, for goodness sake, please stop licking the dog."

"Why?!?"

Now, in those moments, even if I could explain to her the biological workings and benefits of broccoli to her five-year-old body, which I can't, or even if I could explain to her the way electricity works (discovered in 1752 by Benjamin Franklin . . . something about a kite in a thunderstorm and now we have electrons passing through copper wires),[5] which I (obviously) can't . . . but even if I could explain these things with eloquence, her cute little five-year-old face would just look back up at me and say . . .

"*Why?*"

And so I ask (in my best Paisley voice), "Why?"

Why does she ask "why"?

Certainly some of it is just genuine, unadulterated curiosity. But much of it stems from her desire to insist upon her own way, and more foundationally, it comes from her doubt.

If she really believed that I was wiser than her—if she knew 100 percent that I really loved her and only sought her happiness—she would say, "Okay, Dad."

And sure, there would be times where I'm sure she would still ask "why." She might even express some reluctance. But, she wouldn't pout and seethe and writhe with anger. She would be grateful.

Am I a perfect dad? No way. But when I give my daughter any command and she asks me "Why?" the answer that I almost always give to her—and should always be able to give to her—is, of course, "Because I love you."

That's why.

That's why I'm telling you the things I'm telling you—to eat your broccoli and not hit your sister—because I want you to flourish in every way.

Because I want you to *live*.

Doubt (The Reason for Pursuit)

Let's look at the first sin again. Why did Eve bite that apple hook? Did Satan persuade her with all the positive, future results of her putting fruit between her molars?

No.

He essentially said, "Did God just give you tons of rules? Man, He's really strict, holding out on you. There is more to be had—more happiness apart from your tightfisted God and all his commands."

Adam and Eve let that poison go through their ears and into their hearts.

They lived in a world of "yes," with one "no." One "no"!

And Satan made them believe that God is a God of "no." He made them believe, and makes us believe, the lie . . . still today:

God isn't good.

God doesn't love you.

And they fell. And we fall.

Sin is simply a result of this: We have lost a vision of the glory of the goodness of God. We are blind to who He is.

He is a God of yes.

He is only good.

He is always good.

But we doubt this, and *therefore* we sin.

Sin says to the unchanging, smiling face of God, "I don't really think you want me to be happy."

It says to the One who has sung over us while we sleep, "I don't really think you love me."

Sin is the fruit of doubting the goodness of God.

In whatever "style" we sin, the reason behind the sin is the same: doubting the goodness of God. Ultimately, stiff religious people and secular irreligious people both see God as a taskmaster and Christianity as chains.

Imagine with me . . . God puts Adam and Eve in the garden. He tells them they can do anything they want, literally anything, except they just can't eat from this one tree. Furious, they immediately run away as fast as they can.

What?!?

This is the *irreligious type*.

The irreligious man is more obvious and outspoken about his doubts. He's the prodigal.

He says things like, "Give God 10 percent? Why should I?! It's my money." "No sex?!? Don't think so, sorry. See ya!"

All he sees is chains. Arbitrary rules. Strictness.

He doesn't see that God is bubbling over with joy. He doesn't see that God is good—that in His law He is teaching him the beauty and joy of generosity and the pleasure and dignity of being a one-woman man.

And so he runs from these "chains."

Insane.

Now imagine with me . . . God puts Adam and Eve in the garden. He tells them they can do anything they want, literally anything, except they just can't eat from this one tree. Immediately they begin vehemently pacing around that "bad tree."

"Don't eat the fruit . . . don't eat the fruit . . . don't eat the fruit."

What?!?

This is the *religious type*.

The religious man also sees Christianity as chains, but he doesn't run from the chains. He wears them. This is the older brother.

The religious type doesn't want to tithe just as much as the irreligious secularist. He does it because he has to—he does it in order to get God on his side . . . or maybe so he can feel superior to others.

He is much more chaste, at least outwardly, but it's not because He loves God. It's so he can *feel* righteous, more righteous than other worldly people.

He's always thinking about himself and how he's obeying God's rules, not God or other people.

He doesn't see that God wants him to be happy and free. He sees God as a tight-fisted taskmaster. He doesn't understand that God is good.

And so he wears these "chains."

Insane.

Both of these views reveal an inaccurate, distorted view of God. They reveal what 2 Corinthians 3 tells us, that a veil of doubt prevents all of us from seeing the goodness of God in the face of Christ.

Let's think about this veil for a moment.

Have you ever had a person really angry and bitter with you about something that you did, but they can't seem to forgive you? I have, and have also been guilty of this myself.

Note when this happens, though, especially if there continues to be interaction, the angry person is not only mad about the thing that happened, they also seem to be mad and suspicious *about everything that happens from that point forward.* They interpret everything through the lens of their bitterness.

If you try to do something genuinely nice for them, they view it as condescending pity, charity for the poor.

If you look at them wrong they snap.

It's as if there's a *veil* over their eyes.

Sometimes even if you try to reconcile with them—to apologize—they can even view *that* as you trying to get the upper hand.

Where does this bitter cycle end?!?

I'll tell you where it ends. It ends with blood.

It ends when you demonstrate to this person so much kindness, and they demonstrate to you so much blindness, that they mistreat you. Mock you. Spit on you. Wound you.

Sometimes this is the only thing that will sober them to reality.

We were that really bitter, angry person. We were so malicious, and God was so gracious. We were so blind, and God was so kind. The only thing that would sober us from our drunkenness of doubt was blood.

We would never have awakened to reality until we saw blood. Until we saw the intersection of our sin and God's mercy. Until we saw the cross.

Imagine if my wife only focused on my "rules"?

What if after we got married she said to me, "Okay, so how many times a day do I have to kiss you? How many conversations do we need to have per week? Three? Five? How often do I have to cook for you?"

What would my response be?

Probably stunned silence, and then I'd probably say, "I just want you to love me."

That is all God wants.

The question underneath everything is this: Do we believe God is good?

If we did, we would obey Him. Joyfully.

If we did, we would flourish under his jovial reign.

But we don't. We grumble. We complain. We rebel.

We are suspicious of our God, who continually makes His abundant goodness pass before us doubting Thomases.

The Blazing Center (The Pursuit: Part 5)

Grief suddenly surging upon His frame, "We should depart."
A place to pray.
"Watch and wait."
He steps away.
To the place where men are broken and men are made. The Crucible.
Gethsemane.
Heart beating. Faster breathing. Panic seizing. Falling, weeping. Sweating, heaving. Terror, bleeding. Desperate, screeching. Begging, pleading.
"My Father!"
Behold.
What are we seeing?!?
A God weeping?
A King pleading?
Listen.
A Lamb is bleating.
Love exceeding.
We beheld His glory before, but now what is this glory we are seeing?
This brightness shining?
Can what is pure be refined? He was glorious before, but now what is this sight?
The veil pulled back.
Unapproachable light.
See Him.
The One who uttered the world now speechless.
The One who showed all His wonders in Egypt, who conquered their armies now curled up like a fetus.
See Him.
The One who slept through a storm now sleepless.
The One who walked in the garden of Eden now crippled and broken in sorrow and weakness.

See Him.
The One who was there in the furnace of fire, who came down
on Carmel, shut the mouths of lions now whimpering, crying.
The One who burned in the bush with such glory.
The One who parted the waters now drowning.
The Trinity's second member, abandoned.
For you.
See His glory shining.
Now rising.
The torches approaching. The torture ensuing.
A poison kiss.
Face of flint.

Where the Doubt Lives

You might be thinking, *I'd like to dive in headfirst. I'd love to*
try to give God everything, to really do this "Jesus thing," to
really serve the poor and devote myself to the church and to
reaching out.

I'd live for God—I mean, I really would, but look at my cir-
cumstances. Life has just not gone my way.

I mean, I really would trust God if He would just answer
this prayer, or if He would just finally come through for me. I
think I really would believe if I could just get a sign, something
I could hang my hat on, something that would erase all doubt.

Well, here it is . . .

The cross.

This is the blazing center of the glory of God.

The cross erases all doubt.

In the cross, our hearts find what they have longed for—the
pursuit that can melt our doubt into a puddle of certainty.

Doubt His goodness now, and you will see bruised, blood-
filled eyes gazing at you—not in displeasure but in passion.

Fire.

Reaching for your happiness. Dying for it.

This is where the veil is lifted. How cynicism's head gets crushed flat.

And we all with unveiled faces beholding as in a mirror the glory of the Lord are being changed from one degree of glory to another.

And yet doubt lives on, like a dying murmur. For some reason we continue to ask, "Why?"

What about all those difficult commands, God? Take up my cross?!? I don't get it! I don't want to! "Why?"

Answer?

Blood.

Thorns.

Look at the cross.

See your savior groaning in agony for you . . . see the Father's unending love for you . . . and know that every one of his commands are for your joy.

"Die to yourself."

"Take up your cross and follow me."

"Make disciples of all nations."

"Give up all your possessions."

These commands can't be the handcuffs to your happiness. Look at Him bleeding there. Forgiving the world. Forgiving you. Does this kind of Father give arbitrary commands?

Fall in the dust. Repent. He loves you. Carry your cross. Trust Him when it's hard. Eat your broccoli.

The commands of a Father like this could never be your bondage, only your freedom, only your refuge.

"What about all those unanswered prayers, God? What about me finally getting what I want? Why?"

Answer?

Nails.

Shame.

Look at the cross. Behold the Uncreated, Unrecognizable One, hanging there in your place, and remember His words:

What man is there among you who, when his son asks for a loaf, will give him a stone? Or if he asks for a fish, he will not give him a snake, will he? If you then, being evil, know how to give good gifts to your children, how much more will your Father who is in heaven give what is good to those who ask Him!

Matthew 7:9–11

How much more!

Look at His torn and battered flesh, and know that He will answer your every request with infinite tenderness and wisdom.

Hear Him groaning in agony, and know that if you ask Him for bread, He will give it, and if you ask Him for a stone, *He will not give it.*

Hallelujah!

I have asked God for so many stones and snakes in my life and He has only given me bread. Hallelujah, what a Savior!

Fall in the dust and know you are loved and that whatever you have is exactly what you need.

Remember this, had any other condition been better for you than the one in which you are, Divine Love would have put you there.[6]

Spurgeon

"What about all my pain? Why, God? It's not fair. Why?"

Answer?

Golgotha.

Forsaken.

Look at the cross.

See the One who not only understands your suffering but has experienced infinitely more.

"My God! My God! Why have you forsaken me?!?"

Hear the shrillness of His voice as He suffocates on His own blood.

I do not want to make light of your pain. It is real and it is deep and we will never understand what it all means. But now we know what it *can't* mean.

It can't mean He doesn't love you.

Look at Jesus.

Bearing the wrath of God for you.

Know now, dear child of God, that every trial you face can only be the medicine of a Good Physician—little treatments for your idolatrous soul. Every affliction you meet is the tangible mercy of God loosening your grip on such a fleeting world. Your misfortunes are all mercy.

See Him, and know that they could not be anything else.

See how heaven ordered such deep pain for the salvation of the world and for your soul, and know that if His deepest pain will never be wasted, neither will yours.

Look at the cross and know that because of the cross, you will never suffer as much as you *should.*

"Why this? Why now? Why me? What about . . . ?"

Why have you forsaken me!

If we see Jesus screaming "why" in our place, we will never scream "why" again in despair, only in wonder.

Why would you love me? *Why* would you die for me? Why?

He who did not spare His own Son, but delivered Him over for us all, how will He not also with Him freely give us all things.

Romans 8:32

Why, Lord? Why?!?

Do you see? This is what melts the heart.

The blazing center—the cross.

See the glory. Be changed. Now.

The Blazing Center (The Pursuit: Part 6)

Thrown to the ground like a piece of meat.
"I lay it down of my own accord."
Pushed and mocked. "Hail to the King."
He uttered not a word.
Punched repeated. Kicked mistreated. Wounded flogged and
torn and beaten. Innocent see Him. Called no legions to his side.

That whip was mine. My sin, my pride.
Mutilating the magnificent Christ.
And His glory shined.
As the beatings ensued. He was chewed.
A crown with thorns the size of daggers pressed down toward
the eyes of Yeshua.
A thirty-three-year-old grown man, and He could not stand
as the pain of the cracking whips kept coming.
Blood spraying all over the place now running
into puddles of mercy
His muscles were dirty
And He lay and cried.
See Him.
As the torturers blind took Him away to the place of the
skull.
And there for a moment time stood still
As the one who denied Him three times caught a glimpse
of the Unrecognizable Face
of flint
and he squints
and we squint
As Glory prepares for the final sprint.

God's Goodness and Our True Repentance

Paul expresses 2 Corinthians 3:18 in another way in the second chapter of Romans when he says simply it is "the kindness of God [that] leads you to repentance" (v. 4). This is not what the human heart expects. We expect to hear it is the wrath of God, or the justice of God, that leads us to repentance. But this will not do. The law exposes the disease, the gospel gives the remedy. The goodness of God, and that attribute specifically, is really the medicine that begins to heal the sickness of our idolatry and unbelief.

In his sermon "Removing Idols of the Heart," Tim Keller echoed this sentiment when he said the way to actually destroy the power of a sin is to take it to Mount Calvary, not to Mount Sinai.

> If you take a sin to Mount Sinai that means you're thinking about the danger of it. You're thinking about how it has messed up your life. You're thinking about all the punishments that are probably going to come down on you for it. That is not repentance; that is self-pity. Self-pity and repentance are two different things.
>
> Self-pity is thinking about what a mess your sin got you into. Self-pity is thinking about the consequences of it, what a wreck it's made of you, how God will probably get me for it, or how my parents will probably get me for it, or how my boss will probably get me for it, or all the problems it will create in my life or already has created in my life. "Oh, Lord, how sorry I am this has happened. Oh, Lord, get this out of my life." What you're really doing is saying, "I hate the consequences of this sin," but you haven't learned to hate the sin. You're hating the consequences of the sin, and you're hating yourself for being so stupid.
>
> Self-pity leads to continuing to love the sin so it still has power over you, but hating yourself. Real repentance is when you say, "What has this sin done to God? What has it cost God? What does God feel about it?"[7]

Do you see the difference? Religion, in the end, is totally power-less because it's still all about me. When we look outside ourselves and see the kindness of God and what our sin did to Jesus, that begins to melt us. That begins to change us. The old Puritan Stephen Charnock said it this way:

> A false, religious conviction of sin arises from a consideration of God's justice chiefly, but a true gospel conviction of sin arises from a sense of God's goodness. A religiously convinced person cries out, "I have provoked a power that is like the roaring of a

lion. . . . I have enraged the One that is the Sovereign Lord of heaven and earth, whose word can tear up the foundation of the world. . . ." But a gospel-convinced person cries, "I have profaned the goodness that is like the dropping of a dew. I have offended a God that had His hands stretched out to me as a friend. My heart must be made of marble. My heart must be made of iron to throw His blood in His face."[8]

The Blazing Center (The Pursuit: Part 7)

A beam laid on His freshly plowed back and shoulder.
He carried our shame. Our idolatry boulder.
Three hundred yards up a hill.
"Not my will."
The joy set before Him.
But work left still.
Nails were driven.
"Father, forgive them."
Lifted to heaven completely abandoned.
"My God, my God, why?!?"
His voice was pathetic.
And they jeered and they laughed and they called him a heretic.
A phony.
But there was true Glory. Terrible and blinding.
A glory so bright and shining no torture could scribble it out.
Look now.
This is Calvary. Where humanity's prayer of longing for glory
was answered once and for all
in one fell swoop as God said,
"I will make all my goodness pass before you."
Lift your face. Don't look away.
As He suffers to raise His tattered frame
He arches His back
takes a difficult breath

and says,
"It is finished."
And He bowed His head.
And darkness covered all the land.
And against the backdrop of grossest evil
Glory shone like the sun, with no impedance.
Salvation had come, and sweet forgiveness.
It is finished.
It is finished.
Behold the Lamb
God's only Son.
The race is run.
The work is done.
It is finished.

Idolatry and "It Is Finished"

When we come to the cross and truly see the glory of God in the face of Christ, our lives are reoriented around this vision like planets around the sun.

Our idols are replaced.

Money, work, sex, ego . . . are no longer blazing at the center of all things—Jesus is.

This is what gives us rest. We only find rest in the glory of the finished work of Christ for us.

Let me show you how this looks in my life.

Often career/success is a big idol for me. Because of this, I tend toward overwork and envy. I tend not to enjoy today in obsession over tomorrow in the name of getting ahead. I think things like *I just need something good to happen.*

Plenty of good things have happened and do happen for me, but because of my idolatry, I'm blinded to them.

Maybe this resonates with you.

Maybe you think, *I've been working my tail off and no one recognizes me. I deserve something good to happen. All this bad news. When am I gonna hear some good news?!?*

What's the remedy?

The gospel.

Something good *has* happened to you. Jesus groaned in agony for you on the cross. That's the greatest news your soul will ever hear.

Maybe you've been saying, "I've been striving for years in this business."

"I've been the best mom I know to be to these kids."

"I'm sick of swimming upstream. Why does it have to be so hard?"

I've said many of these things myself.

How do you, how do I, fight these things?

With truth.

The wind is blowing, and has been all along. It is the love of God for you.

Fierce. Strong.

A steady gale waiting to open the sail of your soul.

Look at Jesus bleeding on the cross for you. The blazing center.

Maybe you say, "If I just had something to look forward to, I could get through all the drudgery of these dry seasons; I could have joy in the midst of the hard times."

Because of the cross, you DO have something to look forward to: the face of Jesus Christ. And that's more than any promotion. It's what your soul was made for.

Squint (Repent)

The gospel is by its nature offensive.

Many people have a view of grace that is sentimental and sappy, more built on so-called open-mindedness than on real moral standards. *"It's all about love and grace, man."*

That grace is a cheap grace.

The goodness of God—grace—if taught properly, is incredibly dense and incredibly offensive, because the prerequisite for grace is need. This grates at our independence. To get grace you have to get flat. You have to get broken. You have to be nothing.

If the gospel has never broken you, you have never really heard it.

The gospel says that you are irreparably sinful. You couldn't manage your sex habit. You couldn't stop lying. You tried and failed. You couldn't love anything but yourself. You couldn't change, nor did you really want to. You weren't a victim; you *loved* your sin-cancer. You were so lost . . . so blind. . . . so dead . . .

Now grace.

But God loved you anyway.

The cross.

And now, if you will confess your utter brokenness, your total blindness, if you will repent and make the goodness of God your only hope, if you will really look . . .

You will live.

Do you see?

Jesus is the sun, not a 40-watt light bulb. He is polarizing. He demands everything.

Like He did with Abraham, He asks us to raise our knife to our favorite, dearest idols.

He is staggeringly bright. When we see something truly bright, our first instinct is to cover our eyes and turn away. And sadly, that is our first instinct with Jesus.

Because of sin, when many people truly hear the gospel—the call to take up a cross, the call to die to self, to submit—they squint, then turn back to their comfortable 40-watt idol.

Jesus is too dazzling. For all of us. Everyone squints.

I just want to urge you. Surrender. Trust. He is good. Stay.

Don't look away.

Look and live.

5

Let My Eyes Adjust

Our whole business in this life is to restore to health the eye of the heart whereby God may be seen.

Augustine

> Come behold the wondrous mystery
> In the dawning of the King
> He the theme of heaven's praises
> Robed in frail humanity
> In our longing, in our darkness
> Now the light of life has come
> Look to Christ, who condescended
> Took on flesh to ransom us
>
> "Come Behold the Wondrous Mystery"
> from the *Look & Live* album

I'm a huge fan of classical music. Huge fan. Really.

I love the greats—Bach, Beethoven, Mozart, Brahms, and the list goes on. When I listen to the music composed by these men, it feels as though I'm swept up to another place. Another world. The harmony, the intricacy, the ecstasy, it can at times seem too much. The dynamic range is massive, and therefore mirrors real, raw human emotion and experience.

Classical music by the greats awakens wonder, and much of it is (in my humble and accurate) opinion, art with a capital A. Contemporary pop music, on the other hand, is quite different.

The pop-song genre itself, in its essence, is already less sophisticated than the classical styles of old. On top of that, much of what we hear on modern pop radio today can be summed up as a gross, redundant lyric set to a droning kick drum. Cheap words, cheap melodies, big money. These three-minute tracks aren't meant to lift your mind to higher realities, they're meant to numb your mind to all reality.

The symphony classics of old live on like a fine wine, while these pop songs are the musical equivalent of a Red Bull. A musical Pixy Stix.[1]

I'm not here to start a debate about what is art and what isn't. So let me be clear: There are many pop songs written by people over the last century, and even the last year, that I would absolutely deem as works of art. I actually think a well-written bubble-gum pop song can serve a simple, playful, and noble purpose.

My point is simply this: I have friends who only listen to modern pop-radio. And when those people sit down to listen to a Brahms' requiem or Bach's Mass in B Minor, this is what happens. They listen for fifteen seconds and say, "I don't get it."

Why?

Because it's too much. Too sophisticated. Too transcendent.

They've lived on a steady diet of Ke$ha and Kanye, and now they don't know what to do with Bach.

Our relationship with God works the same way.

So often, we live on a steady diet of the candy-coated bubble-gum pleasures of this world.

We live for sex, money, fame.

We worship in sports stadiums and stand bored in church.

We dink around on our iPads more than we pray.

And when we live like this, when we have lived our entire lives like this and then sit down to open our Bibles, what happens?

We read for three minutes, and we say, "I don't get it."

Why?

Is it the Bible's fault?

No.

It's too much for us. God's glory is bright. It's sophisticated. It is capital-A art. The gospel has depths that we will plumb for the rest of eternity, so we shouldn't expect to get it all in one glance. It's much too bright. Too much.

We have to let our eyes adjust.

Let's begin this chapter by looking at 2 Corinthians 3:18 again: "But we all, with unveiled face, beholding as in a mirror the glory of the Lord, are being transformed into the same image from glory to glory, just as from the Lord, the Spirit."

As I said earlier, this passage tells us that we are changed by a vision of glory. This happens in an on-the-spot kind of sense (we *are* transformed), but it also happens slowly.

Notice the verse says we are transformed "from glory to glory." Some translations say "from one degree of glory to another." In other words, spiritual growth is like physical growth. You can't tell a child is growing right in front of you, but if you see him or her once a year, you will notice a difference.

This verse is essentially about sanctification.

Sanctification is a churchy word that simply means the process of becoming more like Jesus. *Justification* means that we are saved, *sanctification* means that we are being saved, and *glorification* means that we will be saved.

What I want to propose in this chapter is that if justification is about looking, sanctification is about staring.

We grow in Christ not by moving past the gospel, but by gazing deeper into it.

Look and live.

Sounds pretty straightforward, right? Not so fast.

Looking again at 2 Corinthins 3:18, Paul chose the word *beholding*, which must be significant.

To behold is more than to look.

When John the Baptist saw Jesus as he was baptizing people, he did not say, "Look! the Lamb of God." He said, "Behold! the Lamb of God."

Again in John's writings—1 John 3:1—the apostle gets swept up into a moment of worship. In the King James translation, it reads, "*Behold*, what manner of love the Father hath bestowed upon us. . . ."

The most common Old Testament Hebrew word for *behold* is *chazah* or *raah* (about 1,300 times). The word means "to perceive, look, prophesy, to see as a seer in the ecstatic state, perceive with the intelligence, or to see by experience."

The most common New Testament Greek word for *behold* is the word *idou* (about 800 times). That word bids the reader "to attend to what is said, to perceive with the eyes, notice, discern, discover, to turn the eyes, the mind, the attention to something, to pay attention, observe, to inspect, examine, behold."

So, this is more than seeing. More than looking.

It is meditating. Marinating. Examining. Savoring.

We look at a light bulb in our house, but we behold a sunset.

We look at a website, but we behold a Rembrandt.

We eat a McDonald's hamburger. We savor a bacon-wrapped filet mignon cooked Pittsburgh style with blue cheese crumbles.

Beholding is the kind of looking that will change us, but this kind of looking will not be easy.

The Lost Art of Beholding

We live in the most fast-paced, work-obsessed, information-obese, nonstop culture that has ever existed. The twenty-first century is an incubator of hysteric busyness. No facts or metaphors are needed to drive home the point. (By the way, my intention here is not to throw stones, but to observe the reality.)

Where former cultures prided themselves on family and geographical loyalty, our modern culture prides itself on fluidity and independence. We go from place to place, from thing to thing, from dream to dream, and we can plan it all and do it all from a smartphone.

We literally have the world at our fingertips, and while this provides many inherent advantages, it also has massive disadvantages.

If we want to learn how to build a car, we don't have to pay money and take a class anymore. We have YouTube. If we want to write a letter to someone, we type and click Send.

We can learn about anything, but this is precisely the problem. Value lies in scarcity, and because information is in such great supply, it is in little demand. It is devalued. It is water.

But the problem goes deeper than this. In social scientist Herbert Simon's article "Designing Organizations for an Information-Rich World," published in 1971, he made this prophetic observation:

> In an information-rich world, the wealth of information means a dearth of something else: a scarcity of whatever it is that information consumes. What information consumes is rather obvious: it consumes the attention of its recipients. Hence a wealth of information creates a poverty of attention.[2]

What Simon is saying here is that we are not merely devaluing information. We are devaluing ourselves.

We have cultural ADD—a poverty of attention, a complete societal inability to stabilize ourselves upon one thing.

Why?

Because we like our options.

We are Jacks-of-all-trades and masters of none.

Where former cultures were forced to live in one place and children took up the family business, we, on the other hand, can go anywhere, do anything, learn anything.

And because we have been mastered by the overwhelming plethora of options, we stand like a confused kid in a fast-food line.

We marry later and mature later. Where former cultures knew a whole lot about a few things, we know very little about everything. It's like the difference between a river and a swamp. One has boundaries, one can go anywhere. One is alive, one is dead.

Twitter, Facebook, laptops, iPhones, iClouds, iMe, iNoise, blah, blah, blah. A swamp of distraction, not a river of focus. But we need to take this swampy, attention-deprived sickness one level deeper.

What we have just discussed is only an outward cultural manifestation of an inward spiritual reality. What we really have is an ADD of the soul.

We cannot focus on God. We cannot see Him. Our soul is swampy. That is our real poverty of attention. That is the greatest thing we lost at the fall.

Our ability to behold Glory.

To attend God's glory with the full force of our focus.

The reason we exist.

We are too easily placated by constant, mind-numbing noise to sit down with our eyes closed and listen to the symphony—to come out of the darkness long enough to let our eyes get used to being in the Light, where we can actually and finally SEE.

Diminishing Returns and the Holy

Have you ever noticed in the Bible some of the ridiculous things that people worshiped?

In Exodus 32, Moses had been up on the mountain for less than two months, and the people burnt their earrings, made a gold cow, and after seeing God part the waters for them, they said of the cow, "This is your god, O Israel, who brought you up from the land of Egypt" (v. 4).

What?!?

Or what about Hosea 3:1 (ESV) where God said to Hosea, "Go again, love a woman who is loved by another man and is an adulteress, even as the Lord loves the children of Israel, though they turn to other gods and love cakes of raisins."

Cakes of raisins? What are we doing?!?

We are worshiping anything. That's what we are doing.

Green pieces of paper. Social media followers.

We are bouncing from thing to thing and dream to dream, and we are bored to death. It is the law of diminishing returns.

If you have a company that cuts down trees and you have two or three guys working together, you might be able to work very efficiently. But if you begin adding more and more people to the job, the process will not get more efficient but less. The work would become slower, and you'd be paying out more money. Someone would get an arm chopped off.

Your returns diminish.

This is what is happening in our soul in all idolatry.

We keep adding more of our self to something, and the something is not God. We throw our soul at the thing, and we get some measure of thrill from it. But the next time, in order to get the same "thrill," we have to throw more of our self to it.

We need more money. More sex. More applause.

Diminishing returns.

Addiction and idolatry are essentially boredom fighting extinction.

We must increase our interest and investment in the thing, and we will do this until the thing breaks or we break.

The marriage crumbles. The greed backfires. The god isn't enough.

We were made for the Holy. The Beyond.

Our soul's attention is like one thousand laborers that need a task—that crave a task. And the task we were made for is to mine the infinite depths of God—to scale the mountain of His holiness and sing for joy upon every peak.

Nothing else is enough.

Everything else will leave us bored.

There is no end to the hunger of our soul and there is no end to God. He is the only Thing that is always "more."

An ocean without a shore. A mountain without a peak.

The Holy One.

Louis C.K., a unique, modern-day comedian-philosopher, was recently on *Late Night with Conan O'Brien*.

His style is to utilize a clever mixture of humor and the deep human questions, so listening to him is a delightful blend of laughing and aching.

In his discussion with Conan, C.K. explained why he dislikes the culture of smartphones and why he would never get one for his kids. He said that smartphones have taken away "the ability to just be yourself and not be doing something." He continues:

> That's what the phones are taking away, is the ability to just sit there. That's being a person. Because underneath everything in your life there is that thing, that empty—forever empty. That knowledge that it's all for nothing and that you're alone. It's down there. And sometimes when things clear away . . . you're not watching anything . . . you're in your car, and you start going, "Oh no, here it comes . . . I'm alone." It starts to visit on you. Just this sadness. Life is tremendously sad, just by being in it. That's why we text and drive. I look around, pretty much 100 percent of the people driving are texting. And everybody's murdering each other with their cars. But people are willing to risk taking a life and ruining their own because they don't want to be alone for a second . . .

C.K. brings it together with a story about the time he was driving, listening to a Bruce Springsteen song, and quite the emotional experience ensued:

> So I was listening to this song, and I go, "Oh, I'm getting sad. . . . Gotta get the phone and write 'Hi' to like fifty people." But

then I said, "You know what . . . Don't. Just be sad. Just let the sadness hit you like a truck." And I let it come, and . . . I pulled over and I just cried. . . . I cried so much. And it was beautiful.

And then I had happy feelings. Because when you let yourself feel sad, your body has antibodies, it has happiness that comes rushing in to meet the sadness. So I was grateful to feel sad, and then I met it with true, profound happiness. It was such a trip.

The thing is, because we don't want that first bit of sad, we push it away with a little phone or with food. And so you never feel completely sad or completely happy, you just feel kinda satisfied with your product, and then you die. So that's why I don't want to get a phone for my kids.[3]

Behold the Lamb of God

Worship is war.

The call is to behold the Son of God, not merely look at Him.

It is to gaze deep into the gospel, not merely pray some prayer and then move on.

We must linger.

Christianity is the hard, joyful journey of beholding Jesus by faith until the day you behold Him by sight.

The writer of Hebrews gives us a glimpse into what "beholding" means in this famous passage:

> Therefore, since we have so great a cloud of witnesses surrounding us, let us also lay aside every encumbrance and the sin which so easily entangles us, and let us run with endurance the race that is set before us, fixing our eyes on Jesus, the author and perfecter of faith, who for the joy set before Him endured the cross, despising the shame, and has sat down at the right hand of the throne of God. For consider Him . . .
>
> Hebrews 12:1–3

We must not merely look at Jesus, but rather we "fix our eyes" on Jesus.

Why use this language?

Because as Spurgeon said, "Our eyes will not go upward to the Lord of themselves, but they incline to look downward, or inward, or anywhere but to the Lord."[4]

God's Word says "fix" because this is what we have to do when we wake up in the morning. We have to "fix." We have to glue. We have to fight.

Because if I don't fight every day to "fix" my eyes on Jesus, my ADD soul will look to a million lesser things.

Not only that, but the writer of Hebrews urges us to "consider Him."

That word *consider* in the Greek is fascinating. It is the word that a jeweler would use when he examines a diamond to discover its excellence and value. He "considers" it. He holds it up. He roves over every facet of the diamond. He studies it.

This is what Jesus is worthy of.

Not our fleeting glances. Not our drive-by looks.

A steady gaze.

Our deepest contemplation. Our most serious examination. He can handle it. Only He can.

A roving over of His numberless attributes.

A delighting in and exploring of every single facet of our diamond-like God.

We were made for this—to throw the full force of our attention upon God and His glory. This is what Jesus is worthy of, and this is what we must do.

But I want to be clear, this is not going to be easy or natural. It should not be—due to both the nature of the Glory and the nature of the looking.

The nature of the Glory is so ineffable, so bright, so majestic, so deep, that we are blinded by its excellence.

We squint. It hurts.

His wisdom is higher, and we are fools.

On top of this, the nature of the looking is such that we are not accustomed to. Our souls have shriveled.

We are accustomed to a Red-Bull, drive-thru-paced life, and this is simply not how sanctification works. The "looking" will be painful. Sometimes it will feel like wood splintering the flesh.

It will take faith and guts—a willingness to say "No!" to the noise, "No" to the anxious morning pull to white-knuckle productivity.

As A. W. Tozer said, "It will cost something to walk slow in the parade of the ages, while excited men of time rush about confusing motion with progress."[5]

But we have heard this before.

The path to life is through a cross.

It's going to get worse before it gets better. Your happiness is on the far side of your holiness.

Cross then life.

Death then resurrection.

So look. Be still. Behold.

It's worth it.

Martin Luther, in his commentary on Galatians, said: "The gospel is the central article of the Christian faith. Most necessary is it that we learn it well, teach it to others, and *beat it into their heads continually*."

"Beat it into their heads continually" is a Martin Luther way of saying "let your eyes adjust."

In the previous chapter we talked about how a vision of the goodness of God in the gospel is what first and fundamentally changes us. In other words, our salvation, or justification, comes not fundamentally from trying but from looking—from seeing the glory of God in the face of Christ.

But this is also where our continued salvation, or sanctification, comes from. It is also a looking to the glory of God in the gospel.

As I said before, you might say it this way, "If justification is about looking, sanctification is about staring."

Beholding.

We think that sanctification is primarily about effort and sweat, but it is not—at least at a fundamental level. Sanctification is about becoming in practice what we are in reality. Sanctification is really the process of us catching up with our justification.

We have been given so many privileges and blessings in Christ that one glance cannot take it all in. That's like glancing at the Milky Way galaxy. It is too ineffable.

As my pastor, J.D. Greear, says, "The gospel is not the diving board into the pool of Christianity, it is the pool itself."

We look at the cross to be saved, we keep looking at the cross until we die, and then we look at the cross for all eternity.

Our most natural, authentic Christlikeness will come not from our trying harder but from our staring longer.

What Are You Looking At?

"What are you looking at?"

We've all heard and said this phrase before.

When someone is looking off into the distance in awed wonder, you ask, "What are you looking at?" When someone is looking toward your face with a confused, disgusted look—brow furrowed, lip curled—you ask, "What are *you* looking at?!?" Surely it couldn't be your face. It would have to be something much worse.

Funny, though, what we are looking at has a direct correlation to our countenance. This is a biblical theme and one that we all can relate to.

The face is the window to the soul—a billboard for the soul.

If life is hard for you right now, people don't figure that out by looking at your stomach. They see it by looking into your eyes.

If you are delighted about something, we don't see that in your kneecaps but in your smile.

David captured this idea in Psalm 42:11, the psalm of despairing worship: "Hope in God, for I shall yet praise Him, the help of my countenance and my God." And again, in Psalm 34:5: "They looked to Him and were radiant, and their faces will never be ashamed." And in Exodus, when Moses was on the mountain with God, just beholding His glory, Moses came down and his face was so bright the sons of Israel were afraid to come near him (Exodus 34:30).

The point is this: The most consistent expression of our countenance reveals us. It shows what we are looking at.

The Christian is not sad for the long haul. There will be sad seasons, hard seasons. But the predominant theme of the Christian's life is joy.

Joy triumphs in the end. The minor resolves to major.

The point is also this: Beholding is becoming, no matter what you are looking at.

To say it Augustine's way, we are what we love. Our lives conform to our ultimate treasure. We mirror it. We glorify it.

We have seen the positive, powerful results of beholding God's glory in 2 Corinthians 3:18, but the negative results of beholding idols are equally pervasive. Consider Psalm 115:4–8:

Idols are silver and gold, the work of man's hands. They have mouths, but they cannot speak; they have eyes, but they cannot see; they have ears, but they cannot hear; they have noses, but they cannot smell; they have hands, but they cannot feel; they have feet, but they cannot walk; they cannot make a sound with their throat. Those who make them *will become like them,* everyone who trusts in them.

Those who behold idols become like them: dumb.

An idol is something that has left its natural and dignified purpose and jumped into the place of God, thereby breaking.

And that is exactly what happens to the idolater. He leaves his natural and dignified purpose and jumps into the place of God, and he breaks.

If you are "looking at" fame, beholding its glory, you will become like "fame." You will chew people up and spit them out. You will never be satisfied. You will value names in lights over real relationships. You will cover your life in makeup.

If you behold Jesus, you will not become less human but more. You will become meek. You will become courageous. You will become loving, joyful, peaceful.

Because when we behold the glory of God, we are aligning our lives toward their proper goal. We are doing what we were built to do.

Hear these words from Henry Scougal: "He who loveth mean and sordid things, doth thereby become base and vile; but a noble and well-placed affection, doth advance and improve the spirit unto a conformity with the perfections which it loves."[6]

Beholding is becoming.

What are you looking at?

A New Diet

Worship is always happening, and it is always happening the same way: revelation and response.

In order to worship money, we must first have a vision of the glory of money. In order to worship sex, we must experience the glory of it first.

Human beings tend to worship whatever glory we put in front of our face. Whether it's the glory of God or something else.

We worship money when we put the glory of money in front of our face. We do this by staying up late and watching the stock market, rising up early and conquering emails, worrying about not having enough money, envying other people who have more than we do. We "behold" the glory of money.

So how do we behold the glory of God? How do we put His glory in front of our face?

In his book *Desiring the Kingdom*, James K.A. Smith makes the powerful argument that we cannot think our way to God. Merely knowing what is true will not change us, because we are not creatures driven by knowledge but desire. Worship. Sehnsucht.

Smith says to change our desires we need essentially to change what we put in front of our face. "We are ritual, liturgical creatures," he says, "whose loves are shaped and aimed by the fundamentally forming practices that we are immersed in." He promotes creating a "liturgy of life" where we strategically envelop our lives in rhythms and patterns of discipleship that train our desires to hunger for God.[7]

It's like training a person who has only listened to modern pop radio to enjoy classical music. It will take some time, some studying. But notice, the end goal is not the removal of music, nor is it merely the listening to classical music, but *the enjoying it*.

The end goal for all our spiritual discipline and all our hard obedience is the enjoyment of God and His law. We are letting our eyes adjust.

Sanctification is about putting your soul on a healthier diet. Glory.

Think about a diet.

You don't go on a diet so you can feel worse. You don't do a diet merely to deprive yourself of things you want.

A diet is about choosing to be frustrated so that you can be happy. Said another way, a diet is about choosing to be happy by choosing to be frustrated.

A diet is not an end in itself. The end is joy.

This is what both secularism and religion miss out on.

Religious people "diet" their soul as an end in itself. They fast, they say, "Look how spiritual I am . . . look what I'm missing out on . . . look what I'm giving up." But they never stop looking at themselves long enough to enjoy the effects and privileges of dieting.

Secular people do not diet their soul at all. They feast, they say, "You only live once. . . . I can't help what I like," and they pursue pseudo, cheap happiness and self-fulfillment as an end in itself.

Christianity puts them in their proper order.

Holiness then happiness.

Frustration then joy.

Jesus says, pick up a cross, and I'll show you real life.

Get on the diet.

In other words, sanctification is the natural result of seeing Glory, just as the natural result of a diet is feeling better.

But in the same way we do not diet naturally, we do not behold Glory naturally.

It requires effort. We must look.

I don't wake up in the morning just naturally reading my Bible and singing worship songs. I must, with a warlike aggression, place the glory of God in front of my face, or I will not change . . . I will not worship Him.

We must be like David in Psalm 16:8 who said, "I have set the Lord continually before me."

Theologians have a name for the way we behold Glory, the way we grow in Christ: *spiritual disciplines* or *the means of grace*. These are the places where Glory is revealed. Interestingly enough, they are all a way of rehearsing the gospel.

In later chapters we will examine these aspects much deeper, but for now, let's look from a 30,000-foot view.

Scripture

The Bible is the specific revelation to us of Jesus Christ. It is where we see His glory.

We are commanded all over the Bible to "meditate" on the Word day and night.

This word *meditate* is the Hebrew word for a cow chewing its cud. The cow chews the grass, it goes down into the cow's stomach, and then comes back up again. It chews some more, swallows, then it comes back up again.

Sounds gross, right? But this is how we grow in Christ and how we see His glory.

We wrestle with the Bible.

We chew and swallow and chew and swallow and think and apply. We let our eyes adjust.

But we must be coming to the Bible in a certain way.

In the Gospels you have the record of religious leaders who were experts in the law, and yet were totally lost.

We have these people today. I know people who have entire books of the Bible memorized and are complete jerks.

How does this happen?

Well, for one, we could say that they have a veil over their eyes (2 Corinthians 3). But, for two, we could say that they are reading the Bible for a certain reason, with a certain lens, and that lens was perhaps greater knowledge. Doctrinal clarity.

That is not why we read the Bible.

That is idolatry. God as a means to an end.

We read the Bible to see Glory. We read the Bible to gaze deeper into the story of the gospel. We read the Bible to behold Jesus.

Prayer

Prayer is about aligning our will with the will of God. It is also a means of grace—a way that we behold Glory. Look how Jesus taught us to pray in Matthew 6:9–13 (NIV):

> Our Father in heaven, hallowed be your name, your kingdom come, your will be done, on earth as it is in heaven. Give us today our daily bread. And forgive us our debts, as we also have forgiven our debtors. And lead us not into temptation, but deliver us from the evil one.

Notice prayer is not all about God, the genie, giving us our three wishes. That also is idolatry. God as a means to an end.

Notice Jesus wants us to begin with worship: "Hallowed be your name."

He wants us to begin by lifting our eyes and seeing our true joy, our true treasure.

Then after that, we carry on to the "regular" things of life: bread, relationships, sin, etc.

Prayer, too, if done rightly, is a rehearsing of the gospel.

We see Him and His greatness first, see our need for Him, then ask for forgiveness and for the things we need.

The gospel.

Prayer is really all about beholding Glory.

Fellowship and Worship

Fellowship with other believers is another huge way that we behold Glory and thereby are sanctified.

When we fellowship with one another and hold one another accountable, we are massaging the gospel into each other's hearts. We are reminding one another constantly about what is true, good, and beautiful, and helping each other's ADD soul-tendencies to stay firmly fixed on Jesus. We are helping each other learn the selflessness that community demands.

And we worship together. Corporate worship is one of the most beautiful ways we can practice 2 Corinthians 3:18. "But we all . . ."

Together as a body we are beholding Glory and being changed . . . there on the spot.

Corporate worship is all about Jesus, and if it is not about Jesus, it is not Christian worship.

We do not go to church to hear helpful living tips, nor do we go to church merely to serve or merely to exercise our spiritual gifts.

We go to church to look at Jesus.

Corporate worship throughout history has been about rehearsing the gospel as a means of beholding Glory.

The ancient liturgies of the past, and even many modern day ones, tell the gospel story. Essentially, it is a model designed after Isaiah 6.

Worship begins with songs and Scriptures about God's transcendance and holiness. Then it moves to a time of confession and prayer. Then it moves to the gospel . . . the cross, resurrection, redemption. And finally it moves to songs and confessions of renewal and surrender.

Water and Table

Baptism and the Lord's Supper are sacraments or symbols practiced by believers.

They are also another way to rehearse the gospel and thereby a means of beholding Glory.

In baptism, the old man is taken underneath the water and the new man is raised up.

We experience this gospel-rehearsing ourselves when we are born again, and also re-rehearse it through the lives of born-again believers in our fellowships.

There are not many things that are more powerful—more beautiful or Glory-radiating—than the testimony of a person truly changed by the gospel.

In the Lord's Supper we are beholding Glory by repenting and remembering the sacrifice of Jesus.

Jesus said, "My flesh is true food . . . my blood is true drink."

When we practice communion, we repent of our feasting upon fake food and fake drink, and remember what our true Food is: "Unless you eat my flesh and drink my blood, you have no life in yourselves" (John 6:53).

When we place the bread (or cracker) in our mouths and bite down, we are beholding the glory of the One that our sins crushed.

When we drink the wine (or juice), we are beholding the glory of the One whose blood alone can cleanse us.

We are tasting and seeing.

Rehearsing the gospel.

Beholding Glory.

Obedience and Practice

We are fundamentally transformed by getting a vision of Glory, but there is a sense in which we can also be transformed through what is known as a hard, painful, unnatural sort of obedience to God.

That which has the appearance of cold religion.

This, too, can be the source of wonderful eye-adjusting, Glory-seeing life change. This too can be a means of grace.

If there is any lack or deficiency in the gospel-centered movement happening today, of which I have been a glad participant, it is that we have perhaps emphasized too greatly the "beholding" over the "behaving"—the indicative over the imperative.

The gospel-centered guys say, "Look at Jesus, and be changed," and this is right. It is in the correct order and it is beautiful, natural, and powerful.

Christian movements in the past that were cold, religious, and devoid of power said, "Do, work, serve, sweat, go . . . and get better at it." There was no glory, no power in it.

Martin Luther said history is like a drunk man on a horse going from one ditch to the other, and it seems that is the case with us.[8]

What Paul did in his writing was this: "Look at Jesus, be changed, *then* do, work, serve, go." In other words, throughout the Bible we have the commands telling us to look . . . to behold . . . to think . . . to remember . . . but then we also have the commands telling us to obey, in seemingly very unnatural ways at times.

"Cut off your hand."

"Crucify the flesh."

In other words—and this is a very difficult balance to strike, one that I will spend the rest of my life trying to get right—we need to behold *and* we need to behave. Both a revelation and response are needed, and they are best done in that order. They are always to be done in that order if there is to be any sort of real change.

We need to look and work.

See and sweat.

Gaze and go.

Stare and start.

But we can flip the order. We can behave and then behold. But in this case we are really behaving that we might behold.

The greatest motivation for obedience is a clearer sight of God. Jesus said this in Matthew 5:8: "Blessed are the pure in heart, for they shall see God."

In other words, if we fight with vigilance to keep our hearts pure, the reward is a vision of glory, not merely a more pure heart, though you might say these are one and the same.

C. S. Lewis put it this way, "The instrument through which you see God is your whole self. And if a man's self is not kept clean and bright, his glimpse of God will be blurred."[9]

See the motivation for keeping the self clean here?

A glimpse of God.

In other words, we should be a hearer so that we can be a doer so that we can be a seer. Because in the doing there is a sort of seeing that occurs when the doing is done by faith.

When we sacrifice our own happiness for the happiness of another, we gain a clearer sight of Jesus. The cross comes into focus.

When a husband chooses to love his wife when he doesn't feel like it—even when and perhaps *especially when* it feels unnatural—he is beholding how Christ loved the church. When we forgive someone and absorb the debt that they left to us, we are "seeing God" and the beauty of His love.

Appetites grow as you use them.

We should love to obey God naturally from the overflow of our hearts, as this is the by-product of seeing Glory and the goal of our faith. However, we should know that as long as there is sin in the world and in our hearts, until the day we see Jesus and our glory-vision gets unblurred, obedience will feel unnatural.

It was not easy or natural for Jesus to go to His cross, and it will most certainly not be easy for us to go to ours.

Putting God first will feel like a cross.

Denying our flesh will be agonizing at times.

But "deny yourself" . . . "take up your cross"—these were never intended to be ends in and of themselves.

No, the end is Joy.

The cross was the means. The reward is always life.

The reward is always a clearer sight of Glory.

Legalism?

And so you ask, how is this not legalism?

Legalism is when I feel that I am more loved by God when I obey Him.

It is not legalism to obey God even when it's hard because I want to see Him.

It's not legalism when you spend time in the Word even when it feels temporarily fruitless when you're doing it with a heart that cries out, "God, I want more of You!" instead of "All right, I've done my time for the day. Check."

Perhaps a good indicator of whether your obedience is done out of legalism or love is who you hope sees your obedience.

Do you think, *Okay, I did the hard the thing! I really hope* ____ *notices!* (Mom, Dad, professor, husband, pastor, etc.)

Or do you think, *Okay, I did the hard thing! God, if not one single person sees it, that's okay, because I know that you see me. You know my heart, and I want to quietly and humbly obey because of your great love for me.*

Fight to See Him

I close this chapter with one of my favorite quotes from A. W. Tozer:

> I think it would be a wonderful thing if every preacher in America would begin to preach about God and nothing else for one solid year. Just one solid year to preach about God. Who He is, His attributes, His perfections, His being, the kind of God He is, why we dare to trust Him, why we can trust Him, why we should trust Him, why we can love Him, why we should love Him, why we dare not fall short. And keep on preaching on God, the triune God, and keep on until God fills the whole horizon and the whole world. Faith would spring up like grass by the watercourses. *Then let a man get up and preach a promise and the whole congregation would say, "I can trust that promise; look who made it."*[10]

There it is. Revelation and response. Real trust and real change as a natural result of seeing real Glory.

Work out your salvation with fear and trembling, for it is God who works in you.

Fight to see Him.

Beholding Him is the fountain of Christian life.

Make your life one unflinching look at the glory of God in the face of Christ. For that is why you exist.

6

Scattered Beams

This is how our souls climb out of their weariness toward you and cease to lean on those things which you have created. *We pass through them* to you, Lord God, who created them in a marvelous way.

Augustine

> Look to the sky, the star-painted heavens
> Who could deny Your glory, God
> The mountains that rise
> The sea as it breaks
> This world full of life
> It's all just a taste
>
> These are scattered beams
> (but) You are the bright Sun
> These are shallow streams
> (but) You are the Ocean
> These are just shadows
> (and) You are the substance
> We are thirsty
> We are dry

Only You can satisfy
You are the Ocean

"The Ocean"
from the *Look &*
Live album

I have a friend (who shall remain nameless) who is a very godly guy but has missed the opportunity to marry several great, godly girls.

His standards are sky-high, so anytime he gets close to really committing to somebody, he breaks it off because it doesn't seem like she's "the one."

Ah, that Hollywood myth that has crept into our cultural subconscious and stunted the growth of thousands of beautiful, grace-filled, redemption-rich relationships. I always tell him, "Jesus is the One. Find yourself a pretty sinner who loves Jesus, and marry her."

The statement is true: it's all about expectations.

If you are expecting a Christmas bonus of $5,000, and a check comes in for $1,500, you will be disappointed and insulted. But if you are not even expecting a Christmas bonus, and a check comes in for $1,500, you just might shout.

Same check.

Expectations.

It's true with paychecks, it's true in relationships, and it's true in our faith and worship.

In Mike Mason's book *Champagne for the Soul*, he makes this very helpful observation: "If I'm looking for a perfectly clear crystal stone on a beach, I may not find one, but if I look for the crystalline in stones, I'll see it gleaming everywhere."[1]

The essence of idolatry is that we look to the world to give us something it was never designed to give us. Our expectations are too high.

We comb the world for a crystal stone that's not here. We keep trying to make our idols "the one," and they just never seem to live up to the job.

They can't. We must learn this.

But we must also embrace this: The crystal stone is not here, but the crystalline is *gleaming in everything.*

One of the reasons I wrote this book was because of how profoundly and deeply I was impacted by the following quote from a Jonathan Edwards sermon preached almost three hundred years ago. I felt I had to talk about it.

As cliché as it may sound, this quote has changed my life. It's changed the way I look at everything.

And as the years pass, the poetic, metaphorical depth of these words continues to open and ripen the truth to me, which is how you recognize a good metaphor. It keeps going. Here it is:

> The enjoyment of God is the only happiness with which our souls can be satisfied. To go to heaven, fully to enjoy God, is infinitely better than the most pleasant accommodations here. Fathers and mothers, husbands, wives, or children, or the company of earthly friends, are but shadows; but God is the substance. These are but scattered beams, but God is the sun. These are but streams. But God is the ocean.
>
> Jonathan Edwards

I love this quote for so many reasons, but the basic thrust of it is this: Christianity gives us a way of looking at the world that is utterly unique and totally liberating.

Christianity is not religious escapism, nor is it overindulgent secularism.

It's not escapism—we do not run from the world, for God has given us all things for our enjoyment (1 Timothy 4:4). The creation is "scattered beams"—God's artwork, full of glory and dignity.

But Christianity is also not secularism—we do not run *to* the world. We don't feast upon the world for its own sake, because these are just "scattered beams." They are not the sun, and thereby they are unable to bear the full weight of our worship and interest.

To be a Christian means we don't look from the world, and

we don't look to the world. To be a Christian means we look *through* the world.

Idolatry looks at the world in amazement.

Worship, true worship, looks through it in amazement. To its source. To the One who is infinitely more amazing.

More interesting.

These things God has made—these shadows, these scattered beams, these shallow streams—are good. And God is better. This is what the universe is all about. This is the end of idolatry. This is the glory of God.

The World

I want to clarify from the outset what I mean when I say "the world."

It could be interpreted when I say that Christians "do not run from the world," that I mean that Christians do not avoid sin, which is not what I mean.

The Bible gives us different categories for talking about "the world." There is *creation* or *matter* as "the world" (Psalm 24:1), the *culture* as "the world" (John 17:15), and the *people* of the world as "the world" (John 3:16).

Then there is a fourth category of "the world," which means a *disposition of rebellion* against God (1 John 2:15). "The world," in this sense, is what Christians are to be at war against, both violently and redemptively. We certainly must "flee sexual immorality" and all other idolatry with a warlike approach.

So, when I say that we do not run from "the world," I mean that we do not run from it in the first three senses.

The Art and the Artist

Galaxies. Turtles. Poets.

Acorns that burst into towering oaks.

Orange juice.

Mozart. Mount Everest.

Sex that crescendos into a little immortal being.

Clouds that cry and make tulips.

This place that God has made is stunning. It is wild. Beautiful. Actually, it is insane. The work of a mad Scientist . . . a real Genius.

Compare the artwork of every artist who has ever lived to the art of God and you will see their works are mere echoes. Reflections. Imitations. Tributes.

God invented Van Gogh and the starry night he painted.

Jonathan Edwards called the universe and everything in it "emanations of His fullness."

In other words, like other great artists, God did not create out of a lack in himself. He created out of fullness. He created beauty because He is beauty.

Prior to creation, God was so full—so filled with love, truth, goodness, wisdom, and beauty—that He overflowed with stars, giraffes, whales, introverts, and extroverts.

A songwriter doesn't need the song he writes, but he needs to communicate something. That is how and why God created.

As we discussed in chapter 1, all things exist in degrees of glory.

There is the glory of God, of people (1 Peter 1:24; Psalm 8:5), of land (Ezekiel 25:9), and of clothing (Luke 7:25). But God's glory is greater than the glory of His creation.

Heavier. Brighter. Different from. Like the sun is different from its beams. And yet, like the sun relates to its beams, the glory is all *His*. "The whole earth is full of *His* glory" (Isaiah 6:3).

Seeing the world as scattered beams and not the sun keeps us away from overindulgent secularism but also from religious escapism. Interestingly enough, it keeps God away from it, too.

We should make a clear distinction between God and His creation, and yet an intimate relationship should always be maintained.

If you say God and creation are the same thing, that's not Christianity, it's Pantheism. In this case, God is so immanent he ceases to be God. If you say God merely created the world—that He created it and then went back to playing bridge with the angels—that's not Christianity, it's Deism. In that case, God is so transcendent He won't even interact with His creation.

Genesis 1:1 tells us, "In the beginning God created," which utterly and eternally sets Him apart from creation. And yet other passages seem to unite Him inextricably to what He has made.

> One God and Father of all who is over all and through all and *in all*.
>
> Ephesians 4:6

> . . . in Him all things hold together.
>
> Colossians 1:17

> . . . the fullness of Him *who fills all in all*.
>
> Ephesians 1:23

Therefore, God is not creation, but He fills creation. Scattered beams.

Theologians make this distinction with the terms *special revelation* and *general revelation*.

Special revelation is Glory with a capital G.

It is the sun itself. It is God himself seen in the person of Christ, in the gospel, and in God's Word. This is the Glory that changes us, that saves us. This is where we see God's heart.

General revelation, on the other hand, is glory with a lower-case g. It is the beam. Creation. In general revelation, we are "seeing God" in a sense, but also something different from and less than Him. We are seeing His attributes, but not in their full, interwoven beauty. It is not enough to save us. It is a beam, and not the thing itself. An echo and not the sound itself. A few traits and not the Personality itself.

You might say it this way: *Special revelation* is seeing the Artist, and *general revelation* is seeing His art.

Think about how a piece of art relates to its artist. The artwork is certainly not the same thing as the artist. It came from the artist and is contingent upon him. He could make another one if he chose to do so.

It is not as valuable as the artist.

The artwork cannot communicate the fullness of who the artist is, nor the vastness of his mind.

But artwork always tells you *something* about an artist. It can communicate lots of things—his values, his morals, his emotions, etc. A piece of art always reveals something of the artist.

In the same way, this world speaks of God. It screams of Him. It is not God, and cannot disclose to us the vastness of His mind and heart, yet this world is charged with the glory of God. "The heavens declare the glory of God" (Psalm 19:1 NIV).

Scattered Beams

Why does a sunset awaken wonder inside us?

Why do we flock to look at mountain ranges and scenic views?

Why does gazing up into a star-filled night almost feel like a prayer? According to an atheist, it's all just matter, a fart of the universe.

But according to the Bible, it is *revelation*.

Why do we feel awe and wonder? Because we all know—deep inside—that we are looking at *art*.

For the nonbeliever, creation reveals just enough about God to condemn himself. He understands that God exists and is powerful, but the stars can't assure him that God loves him. In other words, you cannot get to *special revelation* from *general revelation*.

But when we encounter the cross, when we encounter *special revelation,* then *general revelation* suddenly begins to burst with more revelation than ever before.

If there is a candle lit in another room, you might see the beams of light emitting from that room. You might even know that it is a candle that is burning. You see the beams and their motion. But the light is dim.

If, however, you go into that room and look directly at the candle, the beam becomes much brighter. It is not a different beam that you are seeing. But it seems to be brighter, because you are looking *along the beam to its source*, rather than at the beam from a distance.

Creation is this way.

When we merely look at creation, we are bored. We are disappointed. It is dim. But when we look along creation to its Source, it becomes exponentially brighter. It has a source, a purpose.

We can say all of this in this way: If you have respect for an artist's work, that doesn't necessarily mean you will respect the artist. But if you have deep respect for an artist, you will necessarily have a respect for all his art. You may not *like* all of his art, but you will respect all of it.

The problem with trying to get to God from the world—trying to get to special revelation from general revelation—is that we are trying to build a relationship with an artist through his art, which is not possible. I mean a real relationship.

We can learn some things about the artist but cannot *know him.*

In some sense, deep down, we all desire to know the Artist, but since general revelation can't get us there, we become idolaters as we confuse the art with the Artist. Our expectations are too high.

We are searching for Bach in his symphonies, and he is simply not there. His fingerprints are all over it, but alas, he isn't *there.*

If we try to know an artist merely through his art, we might respect some of the things the artist did, but wouldn't respect all of them. If he made something that we didn't like or we didn't think was beautiful, we would easily doubt the artist's tastes or abilities. We would think he was mistaken. He should have done it another way. We might question his character in the darker pieces, or assume he is not wise.

But when we go from specific revelation to general revelation—when we encounter the glory of God in the gospel and are changed, and *then* we look at the world—it is an utterly different process. Now we know the Artist himself. Now we know His personality, His character, His heart. Suddenly, all of His art begins to sparkle to us with a certain extra clarity and dignity.

We understand it more. We appreciate it more. We want to study all his works. We delight in the intricacies.

If we see something we don't understand or appreciate, we do not doubt the Artist, we doubt ourselves. We question our tastes, not His abilities. We begin to see goodness and wisdom even in His more difficult, darker pieces because we know that He is good and He is wise.

Actually, the works that we don't understand become more interesting to us because we assume there is something important there for us to learn, something we simply haven't grasped yet.

Even if we don't like the art, we esteem all the art because we esteem the Artist.

And this is where the rubber meets the road.

Let's say there's a person whose personality quirks rub me the wrong way. It's not merely that I don't like their sins, I don't like them. If I don't know the Artist or respect Him as a starting point, I will be free to deem this person as a nonvaluable, unworthy thing. It's trash. I don't get it.

Without knowing the Artist, I cannot really give Him the benefit of the doubt. I certainly cannot give His art the benefit of the doubt. The artist has not proven himself to me, so I will not linger there. The art will not awaken wonder or curiosity in me. It will not stretch me. I will be settled in my opinion, because my opinion is the starting point.

However, if I do know the Artist as a starting point—if I deeply respect Him and His artistry as a starting point—even if I dislike the person He has created, I will show a deep respect for that person. Indeed, I will study them.

Why? Because I presume that what I loathe in that person is a flaw in me. They are a work of the Artist! My tastes are surely underdeveloped. I must linger here. *What is here? What is beautiful here? Where is it?*

The Master-Artist made this person, and as such, he or she has worth and dignity and value. And best of all, if I study them, I am sure to learn *something* about the Artist.

Let's do another example.

Let's say there's a situation that I am dealing with that I don't like. Life hasn't gone my way. The van broke down for the eighth time this year. I got laid off and haven't had any work for ninety days. I'm suffering.

If I don't know the Artist or respect Him as a starting point, I will be free to consider this difficult time a total waste of canvas— a total waste of ninety measures of music—a waste of artistic energy. It's trash.

I will think it's not beautiful and that nothing beautiful will ever come of it. I will think that it is bad and He is bad. I will be free to doubt the goodness, wisdom, and beauty of the Artist and His art.

If, on the other hand, I know the Artist—if I deeply respect Him and His artistry as a starting point—even if I dislike the situation, I will show a kind of respect for it. A patience in it.

Indeed, I might curse the artwork, *but I will not curse Him.*

I might hate the music, but I will know that it has a beautiful purpose and aim. It is a work of the Artist! I will study it. I will linger until I learn what I should learn.

Why?

Because my favorite Artist made it. I know Him. He is good. He is wise. He loves to shed brilliant colors on dark blotches. I will endure, nay, embrace the ninety measures of musical pain, because I know that *when* measure ninety-one soars into blissful resolution, it will be all the sweeter for it.

I need to make something somewhat clear at this point, and intend to make it more clear later.

I believe that God is sovereign over all things, and I believe if something happens, He meant for it to happen. This includes sin. You can say He allowed it, or say He purposed it, or whatever you choose to say. Either way, it wouldn't have happened unless He wanted it to.

He created what He created: "For from Him and through Him and to Him are all things" (Romans 11:36).

All things would include all events.

I believe history is a symphony, a drama, a painting. As such, and as in all works of art, there is dissonance, there is conflict, and there are dark blotches.

There is evil. There is suffering. Pain.

But these are all beautiful in their purpose even if they are not beautiful in and of themselves.

Is dissonance in music beautiful in and of itself?

No.

Dissonance is unrest, it is motion—a dominant fifth yearning for the home-like resolution of the one chord.

But therein lies the glory of the resolution.

The resolution is more beautiful for dissonance having preceded it. It is so beautiful not in spite of the dissonance, but *because of it.*

The same applies to drama or visual art. Is conflict beautiful in and of itself? No. Are dark splotches beautiful in and of themselves? No. But the glory of the hero is greater when his wounds are gaping and his foe is stronger.

Because of it.

The colors on the canvas are more vibrant—not in spite of the darkness, but because of it.

All this to say, in an ultimate sense, if something happened, then it is good. It is beautiful in an eternal, panoramic sense, even when it is not beautiful in an earthly, immediate sense.

When we encounter the Artist we suddenly begin seeing His glory in all His art.

This is why we cannot truly respect our neighbor if we do not first respect God. You can't truly obey the second Great Commandment—love your neighbor—if you do not obey the first Great Commandment: love the Lord your God.

Because when you look at a person, you are looking at art. You know it and they know it. Sure they might be a work in progress, but aren't we all! You are looking at someone made by God in His image.

Valuable. Immortal. Art.

If we do not first know and love and trust the Artist, we will always show favoritism. We will tend to gravitate toward the music (aka the people) we like and away from the music we dislike. Our taste will be the final governing factor for the love and interest we show, not the inherent value of the art.

This, therefore, disrespects those paintings that we dislike but also the paintings that we like.

Why should we study an ugly painting?

Why should we love our enemies?

There's no point.

In this sense the most common religious world views would look like the following:

Atheism

There is *no* Artist, and therefore the person, or the art, is not really art at all. They are matter.

So who cares? Why show them the time? Why show them kindness? We are the standard. We say what's beautiful and what's not.

Agnosticism

There is an Artist, but we can't really know who He is, and therefore there is no reason to admire Him.

Although we see other people as art, we have seen some good art and some bad art, and from this alone we cannot ascertain the abilities or character of the Artist.

He might be a real master, but He might be insane, and if so, not all of His works would be valuable. Indeed, some of them would not be considered art. Therefore, at the end of the day, in this view, we are still the standard.

If the art doesn't seem pleasing at first glance, we don't have any reason or power to assume that it is good on some deeper level.[2]

Christianity

There is an Artist. We know Him, and He is a good.

We are certain of His goodness and wisdom, even in the darkest parts of life, because of the cross of Christ. He made people, and therefore all people are infused with dignity and value.

This is why "human beings will only be drawn out of themselves into unselfish acts of service to others when they see God as supremely beautiful."[3]

It is specific revelation that brings us to a real regard for general revelation. It is the glory of God in the face of Christ that teaches us to see the stunning glory glimmering in this world.

First and Second Things

It might seem that if Christianity holds the view that we are to love God more than all that God has made, then in order to truly appreciate the world, we should not be Christian.

This seems logical on the surface.

If we truly love science, we should devote our lives to science. If we truly love music, we should devote ourselves to music. And so on and so forth.

But this does not work. The irony of idolatry is that when we enjoy a thing too much we cease to truly enjoy it. C. S. Lewis made this brilliantly clear in his 1942 essay "First and Second Things":

> The woman who makes a dog the centre of her life loses, in the end, not only her human usefulness and dignity but even the proper pleasure of dog-keeping.
>
> The man who makes alcohol his chief good loses not only his job but his palate and all power of enjoying the earlier (and only pleasurable) levels of intoxication.
>
> It is a glorious thing to feel for a moment or two that the whole meaning of the universe is summed up in one woman—glorious so long as other duties and pleasures keep tearing you away from her. But clear the decks and so arrange your life (it is sometimes feasible) that you will have nothing to do but contemplate her, and what happens?
>
> Of course this law has been discovered before, but it will stand re-discovery. It may be stated as follows: every preference of a small good to a great, or partial good to a total good, involves the loss of the small or partial good for which the sacrifice is made. . . .
>
> You can't get second things by putting them first. You get second things only by putting first things first.[4]

Tim Keller gives a wonderful example of this in his book *Every Good Endeavor*. He writes about the famous jazz musician John Coltrane, a very successful musician in worldly standards. Coltrane had a lot going for him, but music wasn't just his job, it was his idol. So he would overwork. He would obsess about how he was perceived. Since he enjoyed music too much, he didn't really enjoy it at all. He was looking *at* music. *At* work.

And then he met Jesus.

Suddenly he started to enjoy music again. Why?

Because he realized music was just music. It ceased to be a devil when it ceased to be a god. He stopped looking at music, and started looking *through* it. It was no longer an end in itself, and therefore he could truly enjoy it. It wasn't everything anymore, and therefore he could relax.

Don't you want to live this way?

Don't you want to just enjoy what God has made and not be enslaved to it?

Don't you want the world under your feet where it belongs?

Then turn your idol on its head. Instead of making it *the* reason you worship, make it *a* reason you worship.

Meat? Milk?

One of my favorite choruses is one that I actually have a small bone to pick with.

> Turn your eyes upon Jesus,
> Look full in His wonderful face,
> And the things of earth will grow strangely dim,
> In the light of His glory and grace.[5]

Now, before you get all riled up, remember, it's one of my favorites. It's really the message of this book.

There's just a small nuance in the lyric that I'd like to press on.

When we encounter Jesus, the Sun blazing at the center of all things, the things of earth *do* grow "strangely dim." He is infinitely brighter and eclipses them all. Compared to Him, they are, as Paul said, "rubbish." And that is exactly what this chorus communicates so well.

However, at the same time, because we are "turning our eyes upon Jesus," the world is also beginning to explode with brightness. With goodness and purpose. With dignity.

Maybe the lyric should say, "And the things of earth will begin to shine in the light of His glory and grace"?

I don't know.

But if we sang it this way, it should only be after we have sung it the first way.

Let me explain.

When I was in middle school, I lined up all my secular CDs on a fence and shot them with a BB gun. Probably about $800 worth of music.

My youth pastor told me that secular music was rotting my brain. In my specific case, he was probably right. I loved music and was extremely impressionable. It had an idol-like power in my life.

Is there anything wrong with music?

No.

But for that season of my life, there was something very wrong with it.

I hear so many stories like this, especially from new believers. Someone encounters Christ . . . they "turn their eyes upon Jesus" . . . and their lives get wrecked in the best way. They get *radical*.

They immediately throw away their alcohol, burn all their movies, stop hanging out with their lost friends, and get all their tattoos removed. And it's wonderful. It's exactly what they should do.

What's wrong with watching movies or hanging out with lost people? Nothing.

But for them, for that season, it is wrong. Right now they are too immature to handle those things, and it is very mature of them to acknowledge their immaturity. Those things were the center, and now they've got to get Jesus in the center.

First Timothy 6:17 (ESV)—"God . . . richly provides us with everything to enjoy"—usually doesn't apply to new believers. This is not because the Bible is not authoritative. It is because of 1 Corinthians 10:23–31:

> All things are lawful, but not all things are profitable. All things are lawful, but not all things edify. Let no one seek his own good,

but that of his neighbor. Eat anything that is sold in the meat market without asking questions for conscience' sake; for the earth is the Lord's, and all it contains. If one of the unbelievers invites you and you want to go, eat anything that is set before you without asking questions for conscience' sake. But if anyone says to you, "This is meat sacrificed to idols," do not eat it, for the sake of the one who informed you, and for conscience' sake; I mean not your own conscience, but the other man's; for why is my freedom judged by another's conscience? If I partake with thankfulness, why am I slandered concerning that for which I give thanks? Whether, then, you eat or drink or whatever you do, do all to the glory of God.

What I'm saying is this: In a way, the belief that we need to get away from the world is an immature view. It is needed for most Christians early on and in some seasons, but really it is milk.

The more mature view, the "meat," is to interact with the world aggressively . . . to exercise dominion over it . . . to enjoy it. But this requires wisdom and discernment.

On Christ's glory I would fix all my thoughts and desires, and the more I see of the glory of Christ, the more the painted beauties of this world will wither in my eyes and I will be more and more crucified to this world. It will become to me like something dead and putrid, impossible for me to enjoy.[6]

John Owen

Is this true? Absolutely.

The point is, some of you reading this right now need to be more radical. You need to take that thing that's distracting you from Jesus (which is probably not a bad thing in and of itself—maybe it's an iPhone, maybe a relationship, maybe some habit) and you need to throw it in a bonfire.

You are overindulging and you need to temporarily escape from this thing. You need to obey Deuteronomy 13 and stone your idol to death.

> If your brother, your mother's son, or your son or daughter, or
> the wife you cherish, or your friend who is as your own soul,
> entice you secretly, saying, "Let us go and serve other gods. . . ."
> You shall stone him to death because he has sought to seduce
> you from the Lord your God who brought you out from the land
> of Egypt, out of the house of slavery.
>
> Deuteronomy 13:6, 10

Others of you need to be less radical. You need to enjoy life
a little more. You need to obey 1 Timothy 4:4, which says, "For
everything created by God is good, and nothing is to be rejected
if it is received with gratitude." Look along the beam. You've
been avoiding God's artwork and you should just enjoy it. Go
on. Look *through* it. It's fun.

Broken by Glory

Most of my life I have understood that I am a sinner who deserves hell. But that's just the problem. I "got" it.

Jesus gives this parable in Luke 18:10–14:

> Two men went up into the temple to pray, one a Pharisee and the
> other a tax collector. The Pharisee stood and was praying this
> to himself: "God, I thank You that I am not like other people:
> swindlers, unjust, adulterers, or even like this tax collector. I
> fast twice a week; I pay tithes of all that I get." But the tax col-
> lector, standing some distance away, was even unwilling to lift
> up his eyes to heaven, but was beating his breast, saying, "God,
> be merciful to me, the sinner!" I tell you, this man went to his
> house justified rather than the other.

The first man in this story is a religious man. He "gets" it.
He understands all the doctrines. He understands that God is
holy and reminds other people of it often.

But does he really understand?

He is totally unmoved by doctrine. His heart is cold. He stands arrogantly in God's presence. He claims to have seen Glory, but he is still on his feet.

The second man is a "sinner." He is not religious, but the irony is that he understands more of God and His holiness than the religious man.

How do we know this?

The Greatness broke him. He beat his chest. He stood far off. He knew what he was capable of and knew what God was capable of and He begged for mercy.

For most of my life I was that religious man.

I could give you all the right answers, but the answers didn't move me. They didn't break me.

But the more I began to stare at the cross—to see the heights of God's holiness and the depths of my sin—the more I began to say with Peter, "Go away from me, Lord, for I am a sinful man."

I began to understand that I am not merely a sinner who deserves hell one day. No, God is more holy than that. I don't deserve hell one day. What I deserve is hell right now. This moment.

What does this have to do with scattered beams? Everything.

Part of the amazing thing about creation is simply that it is. That is truly amazing. But the other amazing thing is that I am experiencing it. Me. A sinner.

This is what opened the door to my real enjoyment of the world.

The gospel. Specific revelation.

Brokenness.

Glory in the face of Christ.

Suddenly I understood that anything I experience in life that is better than hell is sheer grace. It is all gift!

Suddenly thank-yous began flying out of my mouth.

Suddenly friendships meant more.

Suddenly food tasted better.

We see this in movies all the time, don't we? There's a guy who doesn't really enjoy life, he takes everything for granted. Then suddenly in a turn of events, he experiences a deep trial. He gets broken. Then, through some miraculous mercy, he is rescued from the trial and then goes back to normal life again, but he seeing everything differently now. Everything means more.

Here's a test.

When you watch a person skilled at what they do, when you see someone doing what they were obviously born to do, something they have spent hours perfecting—maybe it's a world-class singer or an Olympic athlete—is your first thought, *Wow, they are amazing?* Or is your first thought, *Wow, God, you are amazing?*

When someone does something kind to you, when they sweep you off your feet with a word of encouragement or an act of lavish generosity, is your first thought, *Wow, how kind of them?* Or is your first thought, *How kind of God?*

When you take a bite of a filet mignon, when your eyes open in the morning, when you _____ (fill in the blank), is your first thought, *Thank you, God?* Are you amazed?

If you are not looking at the world with wonder, perhaps it means you haven't been broken yet. You have yet to walk through the trial of God's holiness. It might mean that you "get" God's glory.

But the truth is you can't "get" God's glory.

You can only get floored by it.

Contentment begins when this is embraced: Life is a gift, not a right. I didn't learn to truly enjoy the world by trying everything or achieving everything I wanted, and I will never find contentment by achieving everything I want. I will only be content when I understand what I deserve.

What we must begin to understand is that the gospel deconstructs a man before it reconstructs him. First it teaches him he is entitled to nothing, and then it gives him everything.

Beholding the Glory

We came around the mountain curve, and I was floored.

"Whoa! Oh my goodness. Look at that sunset!"

We curve again . . . out of glory's view.

"Oh my goodness. Hey, guys, did you see that?!?"

I look in the rearview mirror.

(Crickets.)

Every face is illumined by a smartphone. Every ear plugged by headphones.

Perhaps the worst effect of the fall is that we lost our ability to focus . . . both on God and on the world. We tinker with everything and *behold* nothing. We skim beauty.

In the last chapter we discussed how we behold the glory of the Lord. We consider Him. We gaze upon Him in the gospel; not merely looking but marinating, because we typically don't sit down, read two verses, and experience Isaiah 6.

We must linger.

When we behold the glory of God in creation, it is not really a different glory, nor is it really a different beholding. We must look at these scattered beams. Really look. We must study them. Why? Because it shows us something of the Artist.

I heard John Piper once say, "I think C. S. Lewis would have thought boredom with the world is a sin. It insults the glory of creation." I would agree. But we should also say that if it insults the glory of creation, the art, then certainly it would also insult the glory of the Artist.

What insults an artist?

To disrespect his work. To disregard it. To consider it boring.

And what glorifies an artist?

Not only enjoying him and his company. Not only speaking about him, but also enjoying his art. Emoting over it. Studying it. Using it for its intended purpose.

That's what we are supposed to do with creation. Anything else is an insult.

I want to be like G. K. Chesterton, who said, "I deny most energetically that anything is, or can be, uninteresting."[7]

That is an amazing statement. *Nothing is boring.*

Saying and living a statement like that does not require the galvanization of willpower. It requires humility. Wonder demands humility. As Ann Voskamp says in *One Thousand Gifts*, "The humble live surprised."

Those who do not enjoy creation—the art—are those who think they already "get" it.

"I've already seen this," they say.

Yes, but have you noticed these intricacies? Have you noticed how the Artist used these certain colors here and there?

Have you noticed?

Have you noticed lately the absolute silliness of a squirrel?

Have you noticed lately that acorns explode into pillars of wood with Afros?

Have you noticed lately that the word *pillars* sounds funny?

Have you noticed lately that peanut butter sticks to stuff you put it on?

Have you noticed lately that you and seven billion other people are spinning at a rate of 1,000 mph on a globe train that doesn't have a track, and you're not screaming your heads off?

Have you noticed? Are you looking? Are you thinking? Are you beholding the art and the Artist?

Or maybe this is where more of the rubber meets the road: When your spouse tells you a story, do you *really* listen to her? Are you thinking about your career? Thinking about your rebuttal argument? Or are you beholding her, looking *through* her? Are you thinking about the unique ways God made her, and delighting in her intricacies.

When you are at work, are you thinking about just getting through all the drudgery?

Pride keeps us from wonder. Our self-staring keeps us from glory-vision.

"Wonder at reality demands the humility to sit at the foot of a dandelion," writes Thomas Dubay. "The proud are so full of themselves that there is little room to marvel at anything else."[8]

Seeing the glory of God in the face of Christ is the only glory powerful enough to shatter our self obsession.

It is the gospel that gets our eyes off of ourselves and teaches us to live in wonder. It is Jesus and Jesus alone who can humble us and help us see His beauty all around us in everything.

Proverbs says, "The fear of the Lord is the beginning of wisdom" (9:10; 111:10).

There it is again.

When we are floored by specific revelation, the door to wisdom and general revelation is opened to us.

Before we encounter the gospel, we worship ourselves. We are unimpressed with the art and the Artist. Skeptical of the art and the Artist.

Wonder is the real beginning of all learning. Awe at God.

G. K. Chesterton seemed to get "wonder" better than anyone:

Because children have abounding vitality, because they are in spirit fierce and free, therefore they want things repeated and unchanged. They always say, "Do it again"; and the grown-up person does it again until he is nearly dead. For grown-up people are not strong enough to exult in monotony. But perhaps God is strong enough to exult in monotony. It is possible that God says every morning, "Do it again" to the sun; and every evening, "Do it again" to the moon. It may not be automatic necessity that makes all daisies alike; it may be that God makes every daisy separately, but has never got tired of making them. It may be that He has the eternal appetite of infancy; for we have sinned and grown old, and our Father is younger than we.[9]

Become a student of God by becoming a student of the world.

Seeing the world as scattered beams gives dignity to every field of work and study and puts Christ at the top, where He belongs.

As Christians, we do not escape from the arts, nor do we make the arts into an idol. We should do the arts to the glory of God. They are scattered beams. We should study them deeply, we should practice hard, but never as an end in itself. It's just music. It's just paint. It's just a speech. We exercise dominion over it, not vice versa. When we see this, the arts take their proper place and hold their proper weight. The same would apply to science, business, and every field of study and work.

Everything to the Glory of God

Eating tacos. Drinking coffee. Reading blog posts. Cutting toenails.

Kissing your spouse. Mowing the grass. Using your phone. Scoring a goal.

Cooking dinner. Taking a walk.

Writing a song. Going to work. Playing Scrabble.

> Whether, then, you eat or drink or whatever you do, do all to the glory of God.
>
> 1 Corinthians 10:31

Um . . . okay. How?

If you have never been overwhelmed by the command in this verse, it probably means you've either never read it, or never really thought about it.

Read it again.

The command overwhelms for two reasons.

The first and most obvious reason is its radical pervasiveness. "Whatever you do" is everything. That's everything in life, and doing absolutely everything rightly is absolutely and rightly overwhelming.

Second, the command overwhelms because it is hard to comprehend, which compounds the weight of reason one. We don't understand the most life-pervasive, practical, and arguably most important command in the Bible.

How in the world do I tie my shoes "to the glory of God"? What does that even mean? Help?!

I was unsure about this verse for most of my life because I didn't know what "glory" or "the glory of God" was.

But the more I began to grapple with it, the more I found the key. I began reading it like this: "Whether, then, you eat or drink or whatever you do, do all to the *goodness* of God."

And life began to sparkle.

That's what it means to eat "to the glory of God."

Take the filet mignon . . . cut it . . . bite it . . . let the flavors explode in your mouth . . . enjoy every second and know that Goodness made it all possible.

It is grace. It is gift.

Flavors exist because God is good. Tastebuds exist because God is good.

I exist and this moment exists only because God is good.

I should have been like the rich man in hell, saying, "Send Lazarus to dip the tip of his finger in water and cool my tongue," but I'm not. I'm here enjoying a steak in an air-conditioned building.

God, you are too good to me, and I would not trade places with a king. I worship you, Lord.

That's "to the glory of God."

Enjoy it, thank God with all your heart, and tell everyone how kind God has been to you.

That's really what it means to glorify something.

To glorify something simply means to enjoy something and tell everyone how good it is. We do this with music, football, sex, everything.

Let's do this with Jesus. Let's enjoy Him in the gospel—in everything—and then tell everyone how good He is.

How much *better* He is.

I'll finish this chapter where it started.

My band and I for the last two years have actually adopted the phrase "scattered beams" into our regular vocabulary.

It's been a lot of fun, and also a simple, helpful means of "letting our eyes adjust." So when we sit down for a fantastic meal, amidst the sounds of "mmms" and "wows," you will hear one of us wholeheartedly say, "Scattered beams!"

When we're on the road and we see a breathtaking scenic view . . . "Scattered beams."

When we meet an amazing person somewhere who just serves Jesus unnoticed with a smile . . . "Scattered beam."

When we have to stay in a sketchy hotel, or we have to eat fast food because we're short on time, we call that a "dim scattered beam."

Why do we do this?

We're looking through the world. We're reminding each other that on the other side of any good we experience is a greater Good, orchestrating all of it. On the other side of every frustration we experience is infinite kindness and wisdom. We're reminding each other not to overindulge, but also not to escape.

Enjoy the thing to the glory of God. Embrace the thing to the glory of God.

We say "scattered beams" because those two little words infuse every person with dignity, every moment with purpose, and everything with glory.

Try it.

I encourage you to make "scattered beams" a regular part of your own vocabulary. Say it at random, appropriate times in public. Get weird looks from people, and then explain to them what it means. To God the Artist, make Romans 11:36 your prayer: "For from you, and through you, and to you are all things . . . to you be the glory forever."

Look along the beams.

Look at the crystalline sparkling in everything. Have fun.

Be a kid again.

Enjoy it.

Look through this world.

Live wide-eyed and take in all you can.

See the beauty of this place. The wildness.

See the transparency and hollowness of your idols, and turn them on their heads into a reason to worship the true God. Turn your idols from *the* reason you worship into *a* reason you worship.

These are the symphonies. He is the Composer.

These are the paintings. He is the Artist.

If this book has made any sort of positive impact on you, know this: it is a scattered beam. I am a scattered beam. Merely and proudly. I am an invention of God.

Look through me. To Him.

Look and live.

7

Glory and Mission

Human beings will only be drawn out of themselves into unselfish acts of service to others when they see God as supremely beautiful.

Tim Keller

War and hunger filling up this realm
Hurt and anger swelling like a storm
But His grace is strong to save
Hallelujah
There is Hope in Jesus' name
Hope forever

"The Son of God Rises"
from the *Look & Live* album

My wife is a food sharer.

This means that every time we sit down for a meal, at some point during the meal I'm going to hear the phrase, "Mmm. Try this!" and see her cute, smiling face behind a forkful of deliciousness.

Now, due to the laws of nature, I am obligated to eat whatever is on that metal utensil. She's not forcing me to eat it, but as every man knows, she is. It might as well be a command.

If I'm not hungry, if I don't want it, what do I do? I chew, swallow, and smile.

Granted, most of the time what she offers is absolutely delicious, which is precisely the reason she wanted me to try it. *She enjoyed it.*

It's the most natural thing in the world. It's how the world works.

"Mmm. That's delicious!" I say as her smile gets bigger. Because her joy is increased when she sees me praising the thing she has shared. Because joy shared is joy intensified.

That is what missions is all about.

Bubbling, exuberant, pass-it-on joy.

The mission of God is not the handcuffs to your happiness. It is the doorway.

Missions is this: We enjoy God, and therefore we share God, and our joy is increased when we see the nations praising the thing we have shared. After all, shared happiness is the reason the universe exists.

As Jonathan Edwards put it in his essay "The End for Which God Created the World," God created all things, similar to the way a songwriter creates a song. The songwriter doesn't need the song, the song is simply an overflow of who he is that *needs* to be communicated.

God, in the creation of the world and humanity, sought to share His own joy with His created beings in order to have His own joy increased. God loves to see us discover joy in the thing He is joyful in (His own glory), and His joy increases when we praise what He has shared.

Joy shares joy.

But let's be honest. On the surface, this idea that missions is really all about joy sounds dishonest. It sounds preachy.

Think about how the media portrays missions. They usually

highlight the terrible, unloving strategies that feature angry posters and tracts. Judgmental proselytization. That's "missions." We see it in movies, where many times missionaries are made out to be masochistic culture destroyers. Joy is a far cry away.

I even see it in social media. The things I post that are the least liked, re-posted, or re-tweeted, are the statements I make about missions.

"Go to all the world!"

"The harvest is great, the workers are few."

People don't see it as joy or freedom, they see it as clamoring. They see it as triumphalistic. A crusade.

The least-attended conferences in evangelicalism today are the missions conferences.

Our culture, in general, despises proselytization—awkward evangelicals trying to convert them. And I believe that subconscious feeling of awkwardness has crept into the church.

We think missions is for weirdos.

So, what now?

Should we all tell God His methods aren't really working? Maybe He should work on his marketing strategies?

No.

Missions is not this way today because the idea is not true. It is because we are not true.

We need to lean in. Stare longer.

Once again, we need to let our eyes adjust.

Clarifying Terms

The terms *missions* and *mission* are rather confusing.

They are used in different ways by different voices today in the church, and on top of that, the term *mission* has become somewhat cliché, which always adds to the muddle.

Are we all called to missions?

Or are we called just to be on mission?

Is every Christian a missionary, or only the really radical ones who go overseas?

The purpose of words is to mark boundaries, so let's mark some.

What I mean by the phrase "on mission," and what I think most people mean by it, is this: leveraging your time, talents, and resources for the joy of others and the advancement of the gospel, wherever you are. This could include social justice ministry, sharing your faith, or discipling a small group. It could mean a lot of things.

What I mean by "missions" is this: crossing a culture to reach a people who have little or no access to the gospel, with the proclamation of truth and the planting of churches as paramount.

In other words, sharing the gospel with your neighbor in southern suburban America is being "on mission" but it is not "missions." It is evangelism.

Also, building houses for the poor in Iraq is being "on mission," but it is not "missions." It is service. Sharing the gospel with your neighbor in southern Sudan, or planting a church there, I would say, is doing "missions."

As you can see these lines can be tricky at times, as most word boundaries can be. I'm sure you could come up with some exceptions, but if everything is missions then nothing is missions.

Missions needs to be distinct because the need is distinct.

If everything were missions, then we would (or I should say, "will") quickly forget about those who are dying without any way to know Jesus.

We will just keep saying, "Do missions! Do missions!" while we stay where we are, or do nice things, and people in the 10/40 window (or least-reached places) go to hell. (I am not against staying where we are or doing nice things. I am just fighting for clarity.)

For our purposes in this chapter, I will be using both terms, almost synonymously, because my aim here is not to push for one over the other, but simply to show that both "missions" and living "on mission" are both directly related to visions of the glory of the Lord.

Missions As a Result of Seeing Glory

Ebenezer Scrooge, as we all know, was a coldhearted, penny-pinching money lender who lived in London.

Charles Dickens painted the coldness of Scrooge's heart so well. Scrooge hated Christmas, the happiest of holidays. He made his clerk, Bob Cratchit, work grueling hours for awful pay. And on Christmas Eve, hard at work as usual, he would not even accept his nephew's invitation to dinner.

Bah humbug.

Well, that night as we know, Ebenezer had a visitor, the ghost of his old business partner, Jacob Marley, who had also spent his life hoarding his money and gouging the poor. Marley, bound in the chains of his own greed, warns Scrooge that he risks meeting the same fate, if he doesn't change.

Scrooge is visited that night by the three ghosts: the ghost of Christmas past, Christmas present, and Christmas yet to come. In the dramatic visions, Scrooge sees what a selfish man he has been and how his selfishness has wreaked havoc in his own life and in the lives of others. His dream ends and he wakes up, grateful to be alive and a changed man. A generous man.[1]

This is, of course, a fictitious tale, and yet like most good fiction, it is actually truer than reality.

All of us are Scrooges at heart. All of us are all bent in on ourselves, and the only thing strong enough to truly change us—to break our hard hearts—is being swept up into a vision of cosmic proportions.

We don't need to try harder, or get ourselves together.

We need to be shaken.

The only thing that will finally get us out of ourselves is a vision of glory. As we have discussed, this is the fountain of all real, lasting change. A vision of glory is where worship begins, and missions is where it ends.

See, praise, share. See, praise, share.

That is the journey of worship. That is the essence of human experience. That is all we do.

Worship begins with a focus upon some glory that has mesmerized us, and culminates with the sharing of the glory that has satisfied us.

Missions is really nothing but worship that tied its shoes. It is worship that kept going, that continued to its logical conclusion.

See, praise, share. See, praise, share.

Every human being is the non-begrudging, non-awkward spokesperson for that which is his or her true treasure. We praise whatever we behold, and share whatever we praise.

So if you aren't sharing God, then you aren't enjoying God. And if you aren't enjoying God, then you aren't seeing God.

All real missions—the non-begrudging kind—stem from a vision of God's glory. As John Piper has said, worship is the fuel of missions.[2] It is out of the abundance of the heart that the mouth speaks.

Let's look again at the scriptural basis for this.

Worship As the Fuel of Missions

Throughout the Scriptures, when ordinary people see the majesty of God, or the mercy of God, they are forever changed by it, and they go tell everyone about it.

That's just what happens.

Moses encounters God at the burning bush, and the next thing you know, Moses is prophesying to the most powerful man in the world, saying, "Let my people go!" (Exodus 8–11).

The Samaritan woman at the well experiences the grace and omniscience of Jesus, and then she goes and tells the whole town about it (John 4)!

Paul encounters the risen Christ on the Damascus road, and then becomes the greatest missionary to ever live (Acts 9).

You don't get hit by a freight train and stay the same.

There is no text that clearly displays worship fueling mission more than Isaiah 6:1–8 (NIV). Read this famous passage again, even if you have read it thousands of times.

In the year that King Uzziah died, I saw the Lord, high and exalted, seated on a throne; and the train of his robe filled the temple. Above him were seraphim, each with six wings: With two wings they covered their faces, with two they covered their feet, and with two they were flying. And they were calling to one another:

"Holy, holy, holy is the Lord Almighty; the whole earth is full of his glory."

At the sound of their voices the doorposts and thresholds shook and the temple was filled with smoke.

"Woe to me!" I cried. "I am ruined! For I am a man of unclean lips, and I live among a people of unclean lips, and my eyes have seen the King, the Lord Almighty."

Then one of the seraphim flew to me with a live coal in his hand, which he had taken with tongs from the altar. With it he touched my mouth and said, "See, this has touched your lips; your guilt is taken away and your sin atoned for."

Then I heard the voice of the Lord saying, "Whom shall I send? And who will go for us?"

And I said, "Here am I. Send me!"

In this text, Isaiah sees God, sees his own depravity, experiences God's mercy, and then responds in surrender to God's mission. This is the journey of the missionary. This is the missionary's classroom.

But we want to put the cart before the horse.

The tendency of the human heart is to get busy for God before we see God. *The Great Divorce*, a story by C. S. Lewis, illustrates this so well: "Every poet and musician and artist, but for Grace, is drawn away from love of the thing he tells, to love of the telling till, down in Deep Hell, they cannot be interested in God at all but only in what they say about Him."[3]

This is the danger—that we begin to love our "telling" more than the glory we are seeing.

All of us have this drive to "do." It is a good, God-given drive. But it must be tamed. If it is not, as Lewis points out, it will only be a source of self-righteousness.

This is the essence of religion. It begins well. We begin with our eyes on the Lord, and we are serving Him and others for His sake.

See, praise, share. Natural. Beautiful.

But soon we become obsessed with the sharing. Our calendars begin filling up. Soon our eyes are actually drawn *to the sharing itself*. Drawn to ourselves.

And while our worship is "ending" the same way it used to—with good deeds of service, with missions and church attendance and tithing, etc.—the "why" of worship has changed.

Where it begins has changed. The glory has changed.

Our eyes are now on something else, for they will always be on something. They are on us, on our spiritual résumés.

Idolatry.

I used to be obsessed with God using me. I wanted Him to take my life and use it change the world. And I truly think these desires began well.

My prayer life focused on asking God to use me—to fill my calendar with greater kingdom opportunities. Wonderful opportunities. But I was never just praising God for His own sake. Never just talking with Him as an end in itself. I would study the Bible in depth when I was preparing a sermon, but not when I was simply preparing my heart.

I wanted God to use me, but really I was using Him.

Blessed are the pure in heart, for they shall see God.

Matthew 5:5 ESV

Turn to Me and be saved, all the ends of the earth; for I am God, and there is no other.

Isaiah 45:22

So drink. Look first. Tame your busy soul. Do it now.
Behold the Lamb of God.
Then go. Then serve.
It's all the difference in the world. It's the difference between a living faith and a dead religion.
The difference between heaven and hell.

As we have said, beholding the Lord's glory changes us to be more like Him. We become loving, joyful, peaceful.

But that's not all.

If our eyes are on His glory—which is primarily His goodness and His pursuit of us—and we are being changed into His image, that means we are becoming people who are in pursuit.

We go into mission.

The glory of the Lord emanates from our lives as we become the missional people of a missional God.

And this is terrifying.

Because this means God's glory will shine to the world to the degree that I am carrying a cross—to the degree that I am dying to myself.

Becoming like Jesus is not merely about gaining greater emotional stability. It is about learning to die. It is about sacrifice for the good of others.

Suffering for the joy of others. In this, God's glory will be seen.

Seeing Glory As a Result of Missions

So we see the glory of the Lord, and then we respond by going into missions. Most naturally.

But let's remember: *How* do we behold His glory?

We behold the glory of the Lord by thinking—by meditating on the gospel—but we also behold by *doing*. We see the glory

171

of the Lord through giving, serving, sharing. All of these are a means of letting our eyes adjust.

We see God through missions.

Yes, worship is the fuel of missions, *but worship is also the goal of missions.*

This statement, I think, can be taken in a personal sense and a global sense. Let's start by looking at it in a personal sense.

Hebrews 12:14 (NKJV) states clearly, "Pursue . . . holiness, without which no one will see the Lord."

So we should *pursue* in order to *see.* In other words, we should be doers of the Word in order to be see-ers of the Word.

But we should not think of our doing—our obedience and our holiness—as merely the avoidance of sin. That is how I think of it too often. I'm only on defense, focusing on my sins of "commission" (the evil things I actively choose) rather than my sins of "omission" (the good things I passively neglect).

But what does this mean?

It means getting on offense. It means living on mission. It means giving, serving, sharing, going. And *doing all these things as a means of a clearer sight of God.*

These are scattered beams. He is the Sun. He is our joy. Apprehending His goodness, character, and glory is what our souls were made for.

So what does this look like?

Every time we inconvenience ourselves to achieve the happiness of someone else, we understand the love of God a little more. The cross comes into focus.

If you adopt a child, you are letting your eyes adjust to the glory of God's Father-heart—His predestining you and adopting you into His family. You are seeing the cost He paid for your soul. How patient He was to wait for you. How helpless and alone you were and how gentle and kind He is.

If you choose to live overseas to do mission work, you are letting your eyes adjust to the glory of God's willingness to come to our world, to make himself a stranger for your sake.

You are understanding what it is to be misunderstood, to be persecuted for the sake of love and righteousness. You are beholding Glory.

If you sell your car and give the money to a social justice organization, you are beholding the glory of God. You are settling your soul in the truth that you don't need cars or money to be happy. You need God.

If you befriend someone who doesn't deserve your friendship, or perhaps someone who doesn't have very many friends, what are you doing? Beholding Glory. You are seeing the glory of the One who loved His enemies enough to bleed for them. You are seeing the goodness of the God who befriends wicked, undeserving, arrogant sinners—the Holy One who condescends to find things in common with mortal human beings.

Your eyes are adjusting.

Do you see it?

So what does it mean for us to pursue holiness and see the Lord (Hebrews 12:14)? How do we get the Trinity into focus?

Yes, we ponder; yes, we meditate. But we also *do*.

We become like the Trinity.

Essentially, we love.

Love Happening

Our culture is love obsessed.

In some ways this is a deficiency, but in other ways it is most natural. God created love, and love is really the choice drug of the soul.

When my daughters see my wife and me hugging or kissing for a moment, they come rushing in like little magnets, and they always cry out *desperately*, "I want to get in the love!"

I love hearing those words, because those words are why we exist.

We all want to "get in the love."

Chasing fame, more money, our addictions . . . These things are all diversions, distractions, futile attempts of filling our God-void.

We were made for more.

We were made to be swept up into the embrace of the Trinity. We were made for grace-filled human community and all its inebriating unity and diversity. We were made to "get in."

And we see this everywhere.

Listen to pop radio for more than fifteen minutes and you will hear we all want to "get in." Watch a few movies and you'll see there's a societal need to "get in." The most searched word/ phrase/definition on the most searched search engine (Google) in the year 2012 was the word "love."

What is love?

Ask modern science what love is, and it will tell you "love is biology." There's nothing transcendent about it. It's just the chemical synapses of your brain firing. It's hormones. It is the primal instinct of our species to reproduce its own kind.

How romantic.

Ask modern philosophy what love is, and it will tell you "love is nonjudgmentalism, open-mindedness, the acceptance of everything." If he's into guys, cool. If she's into girls, okay. If that's his religion, then it's true for him. If she wants to kill "it," then that's her choice. Don't judge, don't offend, don't disrupt.

How ridiculous.

C. S. Lewis prophetically anticipated this illogical hour in his work *Mere Christianity*: "All sorts of people are fond of repeating the Christian statement that 'God is love. . . .' Of course, what these people mean when they say that God is love is often something quite different: they really mean 'Love is God.'"[4]

We have removed the standard, and therefore, we have actually removed love. So let's look to the Bible and get it back.

The Hebrew word for love is *ahavah*, the root of which means "to give." Essentially, that's what love is: giving. As missionary Amy Carmichael famously said, "You can give without loving, but you cannot love without giving." We see this beautifully and clearly in the two famous 3:16s of the Bible:

> For God so loved the world that he gave his one and only Son, that whoever believes in him shall not perish but have eternal life.
>
> John 3:16 NIV

> This is how we know what love is: Jesus Christ laid down his life for us. And we ought to lay down our lives for our brothers and sisters.
>
> 1 John 3:16 NIV

Love gives.

Another simple way that I like to say it is: Love is *your good at my cost.* Love is a cost to me and a good to you, and it is always these two things together, or it is not love.

For example, I was speaking at a church recently, and after the event ended, a guy volunteered to take me to the airport, about two hours away. He was totally going out of his way, and so I was thanking and praising him for it. He received it, but he soon confessed, "Well, actually, I had to come down here anyway, because I'm meeting up with my girlfriend today."

Oh.

A "good" to me, but not really a "cost" to him.

Not quite love.

On the other hand, let's say this guy had said to me, "Sure, Matt, I'll give up my afternoon to take you to the airport. I'll sacrifice my whole day for you, pay for the gas, but instead of going to the airport, I'd actually like to take you to the mall and buy you some new clothes. You're looking a little disheveled and homeless these days, so I'd love to get you a new wardrobe."

Now, that would be kind, and a cost to him, but it would not really be a good to me, because what would make me truly happy is not clothes but going home to see my family!

Not quite love.

Love is always a cost to me and a good to them. That's what it is.

Given this definition, it is worth mentioning that sometimes the people you love will not see that it is a genuine cost to you. Think the widow's mite. They will receive the good and they will mock or take advantage of you.

But does love require them to know the cost? To understand the cost?

No.

Look at the cross.

Do we understand the cost of Jesus' losing the Father's embrace? No.

Have we ever taken advantage of the gift of grace He has given us? Of course.

And along with this, sometimes the people you love will not recognize that it is a good to them.

We see this with children all the time. You show them love, you give them rules for their happiness, and they think you're trying to take their freedom.

We see this in gospel conversations. You are loving someone's soul the best way you can by holding out the truth for them to see, but they don't see it that way. They see it as a power play. You're trying to win an argument, they think. We see this most of all at the cross, where God was doing the best thing He's ever done, but we didn't see it.

But love is a third thing, too. Love is always a cost to me, a good to them, and a joy for both. It is your good, my cost, *our joy*.

And this truth is crucial if we want to be motivated to love.

Let's look at the scriptural basis for this: It is more blessed to give than to receive (Acts 20:35).

Jonathan Edwards rightly defines this biblical word *blessed* with a word that he coined: *happifying.*[5] That's really what the original text gets at. It is more happifying to give than to receive.

Another example of this is in Psalm 32:1: "Blessed is he whose transgression is forgiven, whose sin is covered!" That *blessed* word there? *Happy.*

Tim Keller puts it this way: "The lack of joy in your life is due to your lack of mission."[6]

It is more happifying to be on mission than to be selfish. This is counterintuitive to the fleshly mind, but it is absolutely the truth.

How many times have I seen this? Maybe you have, too.

Someone gets on a stage at a church with their poorly made slideshow and talks about their recent mission trip to Uganda. They always say something like this, "You know, I was really kinda dreading this trip at first. I've never been out of the country, and to be honest, doing manual labor in the blazing sun every day isn't really my idea of fun. But you know, we got down there and started working, and I saw the kids' faces, and . . . something in me changed. I just worked and served and helped and sweated, and you know what? I've never been happier in my life. Those people blessed me far more than I ever blessed them."

Ever heard that? What happened?

Love happened.

It is more happifying to give than to receive.

Where else do we see this? This famous passage . . .

Therefore, since we have so great a cloud of witnesses surrounding us, let us also lay aside every encumbrance and the sin which so easily entangles us, and let us run with endurance the race that is set before us, fixing our eyes on Jesus, the author and perfecter of our faith, *who for the joy set before Him endured the cross*, despising the shame, and has sat down at the right hand of the throne of God.

Hebrews 12:1–2

The joy set before Him.

The cross was excruciatingly painful. The cross itself certainly was not "the joy set before Him." It was the cost to Him.

So what was the joy?

The joy set before Jesus was taking an unworthy prostitute and making her into a beautiful Bride. The joy set before Him was lifting her and exalting her and seeing the biggest, most joyful and grateful and playful smile sweep across her face. The joy set before Him was living with her in sweetest harmony and matrimony forever.

The joy, you see, was *the joy of love.*

The Christian life is no different for us. We have a cross to carry, a death to die. But like Jesus, the cross is not an end in itself. It is a means. Happiness is the end. That's what the Christian life is about. Love. Joy.

My cost, your good, our joy. In that order.

If you seek happiness, you will never find it. If you seek holiness, happiness will find you.

Christianity does not offer us an easy happiness, only a real happiness. But this is where we get off. With this, we usually fall off into one of two ditches . . .

First, the ditch of total self-denial.

This is the camp that says the cross is an end in itself.

Simply put, this is masochistic religion—all about immediate pain: Do hard things just for the sake of doing hard things. God is a taskmaster; don't enjoy anything.

Others are at the center, but really, this is a disguise. I'm at the center, because in everything I'm doing, I'm just thinking about myself and how hard it is and how awesome I am.

Second, the ditch of total self-indulgence.

This is the camp that says my immediate happiness is an end in itself. Some call this the prosperity gospel. You could also call it secularism. It's all about immediate joy: wealth, health, happiness now.

I'm at the center, and there's no hiding it. God is either neglected, or He is just my genie to give me what I really want. I can sin all I want—indulge—and God's got me covered with Grace. It's all good.

But Christianity puts things in proper order—pain giving way to joy, frustration giving way to happiness.

So lay your idols down. Lay your self-interest down. If you seek happiness, you will never find it, but if you seek holiness, happiness will find you.

The Joy of Good Old-Fashioned Obedience

When we talk about being transformed by a vision of glory in the gospel, when we talk about responding most naturally to a sight of God's goodness with radical sacrifice, worship, and mission, we are talking about what is most true, foundational, and ideal.

Real change happens when our deepest loves and desires change, not merely when we make decisions or try harder. That's the message of this book. But the reality is, in a world of sin and brokenness, in a world of veils and blindness, worship will not always feel natural. Transformation will not happen overnight. Love will not always feel joyful. It will feel like a cross.

We are still selfish, broken people because our vision of His glory is blurred. Incomplete. *"But we all with unveiled face beholding as in a mirror the glory of the Lord . . ."* Nonetheless, we ought to obey Jesus.

This is the sentiment Oswald Chambers expressed: "The stamp of the saint is that he can waive his own rights and obey the Lord Jesus."[7] Just obey. This is a very little-talked-about idea in evangelicalism today. We evangelicals have a category for a natural obedience (worship), and we have a category for an unnatural obedience (legalism), but there is a kind of obedience that pleases God—a hard, unnatural sort of obedience. A "death" to self. And it is not legalism.

How so? Let me remind you: Legalism is when I feel that I am more loved by God because I obey. It is not legalism to obey God when it's hard because I want to see more of Him or please

Him more or be more like Him. Those are fundamentally different motivations.

So we ought to read our Bibles, pray, preach the gospel, make disciples, feed the poor, love the orphan and the widow, serve the least of these, give up all our possessions. And we ought to do all of these things even when we don't feel like it, just because Jesus said so. But when we use our God-given will to do them, we don't do them with self-righteousness but with an aching prayer: *Jesus, thank you for loving me. I want to love others and love you the way that you love me. Help me. Change me.*

I don't always feel like loving my wife. But by God's grace, I love her. I choose to. And in those unnatural, forced moments of blindness to her beauty and blindness to what real happiness is, when I exercise my will and "lay my life down" and just love her, I find that something begins to happen in me. I begin to feel. I "feel" and see her beauty the more I act.

We can say it another way. I don't always feel like singing in corporate worship. I don't. I mean, I've done it as a job for twelve years now, and sometimes I just want to scoot in the back and show up for the sermon. Sometimes I don't want to lift my hands. I've worshiped all week on a stage somewhere, and now I'm just worshiped out.

But you know, there are these pesky commands in the Bible. "[Speak] to one another in psalms and hymns and spiritual songs" (Ephesians 5:19). "Sing praises to God, sing praises!" (Psalm 47:6 ESV). "Clap your hands, all you nations; shout to God with cries of joy" (Psalm 47:1 NIV). "[Lift] up holy hands without anger or disputing" (1 Timothy 2:8 NIV).

So what do I do?

I sing. I worship. I choose.

And something begins to happen. I start to feel. My heart starts to sing. My volition leads or kick-starts my emotion. "Feel this way! This is what is true!" And this is really why we are commanded to sing about God, and not merely talk about

Him. When we sing, we are reminding ourselves of the way we should always feel about God. He is glorious! We cannot merely talk about Him. We must sing.

Jesus said this same truth in this way: "Where your treasure is, there your heart will be also" (Matthew 6:21). Most of the time when this verse is preached, it is said that Jesus meant we give our money to whatever we love—our treasure follows our heart. This is true, but this is not what Jesus said here. He said our heart follows our treasure. In other words, we can actually shape our loves by the practical choices we make about our money. Let me repeat that. We can actually shape our loves by the practical choices we make about our money. Where you give, you care. Emotion follows volition.

And this is why there are commands in the Bible. Because we are still fallen. Because we are still blind. We need some train tracks for our ADD souls.

The Pain of Love, the Cost of Mission

What does awe-inspiring love look like? What is the greatest display of "a cost to me and a good to you"? Substitutionary sacrifice. All the great movies have it.

There is no greater cost to me than laying down my life, and there is no greater good to you than giving you your life. This, of course, is merely an echo of the gospel.

> Therefore Jesus also, that He might sanctify the people through His own blood, suffered outside the gate.
>
> Hebrews 13:12

I went to China recently and met a woman who serves there as a missionary. Her love for the women of China who are sexually trafficked and exploited is absolutely stunning. Awe-inspiring.

A normal day for her looks like this: walking the streets of her city for miles on end, encouraging and sharing Jesus' love

181

with broken women. Going from red light to red light to red light to red light until her head hits a pillow.

At the end of one day on the trip we were praying together, and I'll never forget it. She prayed with such a passion for the Lord. At one point my jaw hit the floor. Along with some tears.

I guess what I expected to hear coming out of her mouth was, "Lord, thank you for getting us through today, and thank you for this team. Give us all good rest tonight . . ." or something like that.

Instead, I heard this aching prayer: "Lord, please give me the strength tomorrow to walk just a little bit longer. Just a little bit longer."

That is a prayer.

I remember she even prayed, "I can't wait to see you, Jesus, but please don't come back yet!" which made me think of Paul and some of his prayers ("I wish to be accursed for their sake . . ." "to stay here is far better for your sake . . . " etc.).

Her love for these women was making her say borderline illogical, un-theological things. But that's what love does sometimes. It makes you crazy.

It walks a little bit longer.

While we were in China, we were assigned the task of visiting some college campuses and sharing the gospel. Our team prayed together, broke up into two groups, and set out. Things were going well until we discovered that college students weren't in classes yet. It was the end of summer. Oops.

What followed was actually quite interesting, though, and proved to be a great learning experience.

Both groups that day showed up to an empty college campus. Disappointed, one of the groups decided, "Well, there's no one here. Let's go shopping." They went shopping and got ice cream and just kinda relaxed.

But the other group (also disappointed) said, "Well, there's no one here. We're just going to have to go find some people." And so they did. They figured it out, and had a pretty good day of ministry.

What was the difference?

The first group's plan was to go to a school and talk to people. The next group's plan was the Great Commission.

That's really the difference between religion and Christianity.

Religion gives us little tasks that we can complete—small boxes to check—and in completing them, we can feel a sort of addictive buzz of self-righteousness. *I did that.* Or in failing them, we can feel a sort of small pseudoshame. A shame that's really not shameful enough.

Christianity, on the other hand, says, "Love the Lord, your God," "Love your neighbor as yourself," "Be holy as I am holy," "Go into all the world and make disciples."

Good grief!

These are not cute little assignments.

These are words that put you on your face. Words that make you say, "God, I need you!" Words that explode our little just-do-enough-to-get-by Christianity to pieces and make us reach for greatness.

Look at the cross.

He didn't give 10 percent, He gave it all. God's love for you will produce more activity in your life for the kingdom than all the little checkboxes in the world.

Worship As the Goal of Missions

Worship gives us the power to do missions, but it also gives us the purpose of missions.

This is found all over the Bible, but it is seen vividly in Revelation 5 and 7. In these passages we see where history is heading. We see the period at the end of the sentence.

What is the purpose of missions?

People. From every tribe, tongue, and nation, surrounding the throne of God and worshiping the Lamb who was slain.

That's the point of missions.

And by "missions," lest we overlook certain people due to our favoritisms, we mean the taking of the gospel to all "peoples." Not simply "living missionally," although that is important. Missions is taking the gospel to every *ethne*—every people group (Matthew 28:19). Jesus is that worthy.

The best way to illustrate how this works itself out is in a story, a true one. John Leonard Dober and David Nitschmann, who lived in Germany in the early 1700s, were followers of Jesus Christ and in their early twenties. They heard about an island in the West Indies full of slaves who had not heard of Christ. Profoundly disturbed by the news and prompted by God, they made preparations to go. More than a year later, with bundles on their backs, looking more like peddlers than pioneering missionaries, they started walking to Denmark, where they hoped to get the church's support.

When they arrived in Copenhagen, the people tried to convince the young men that their plans were foolish. They said no ship would take them to St. Thomas, and if they did make it there, they wouldn't survive the difficult island conditions. Nitschmann answered that for the sake of the gospel, he and Dober would even "work as slaves among the slaves."

When told that wouldn't be allowed, the men stood their ground and said they would work as carpenters, anything, to accomplish their mission. Church leaders were finally convinced and helped the men make their journey. And when Dober and Nitschmann stepped ashore on St. Thomas island, it marked the beginning of a fifty-year labor of their hearts.[8]

The greatest motivation to share the gospel with someone today and every day? Another voice around the throne. A louder song for Jesus.

The greatest injustice in the universe is not that there are people dying of AIDS or people starving to death, even as you read this. It's not that there have been over fifty million abortions in America since Roe v. Wade. It's not even that there are twenty-seven million human slaves in the world today.

These things are absolutely awful. They are worthy of judgment, and I believe they break the heart of God.

But these, even combined, are not the greatest injustice.

The greatest injustice in the universe is that there are human beings who do not worship Jesus Christ.

Now, I'm guessing that, even if you're a Christian, there's something about that statement that just doesn't settle well with you. Something about it makes you slightly uncomfortable.

In our human, finite minds, it is easier to look at any one of these humanitarian/social justice causes and cry out, "Injustice!" than it is to stake claim, in our grossly relativistic society, to a truth that puts us on the outside . . . one of "those people."

God created humanity to worship and obey Him, to glorify and enjoy Him (Genesis 2:15; Colossians 1:16), yet we all have chosen to worship the creature rather than the Creator, who is forever blessed (Romans 1:25).

This is injustice.

God, who is infinitely holy, beautiful, and worthy of adoration, has been set aside by His quintessential creation—recipients of His revelation and bearers of His image—as unsatisfying, unreliable, and at best useful.

This is suicide.

Humanity, through its disobedience, has wandered from the fountain of all joy and life, the worship of God, and chosen to drink from the poisonous puddle of idolatry.

We have abandoned our post and fallen short of glory (Romans 3:23). In not doing what we were created to do, we have become, as C. S. Lewis so timelessly put, "half-hearted creatures, fooling about with drink and sex and ambition when infinite joy is offered us."[9] We have robbed God of glory and ourselves of joy.

This is injustice.

There is a tremendous need in the world today for more people to aid in social issues. We need more to join in the fight against sex-slavery and poverty, more to speak for those without a voice.

But what about those without a song? Without life? Without Christ?

Who will speak for them?

Who will fight for their God-ordained joy in the glory of God?

Starving stomachs must be filled. How much more starving souls?

Who will take God's praise to the nations, for their satisfaction and for God's glory? Where are those who will fight so great an injustice?

The Rarest and Highest of Pleasures

In her 1957 novel, *Atlas Shrugged*, author-philosopher Ayn Rand stated that admiration is the rarest and highest of pleasures. Amazing quote, huh? One you might expect to see in a book like this. The interesting thing is, it came from an atheist.

Even though Ayn didn't believe in God, she understood worship. She understood a truth that we all understand: Our happiest moments as human beings are the moments we forget ourselves in the admiration of something greater than ourselves. Admiration is the rarest and highest of pleasures.

What are the moments you feel truly alive? The happiest moments? When you get your way? When you build your career? When you look in the mirror? No. They are the awe-filled, self-forgetful moments of life—the rock concerts, the football games, the hilarious times with friends—these are the moments we live for. We are the most alive when we are praising some greatness, and, I will add, doing it with friends whom we love.

What is this other than Revelation 5? What is this other than the church, one day surrounding the throne of God, comprised of every tribe, tongue, and nation in rapturous celebration and awe of the Lamb that was slain? This is the reason you exist. To explode with admiration for Jesus Christ and bring as many people as you can into the joy of this admiration.

I will close with these words of David:

> God be gracious to us and bless us,
> And cause His face to shine upon us—Selah.
> That Your way may be known on the earth,
> Your salvation among all nations.
> Let the peoples praise You, O God;
> Let all the peoples praise You.
> Let the nations be glad and sing for joy.
> Psalm 67:1-4

Missions is not the handcuffs to your happiness. It is the door. Carry the gospel to the nations. Carry it to your neighbors. Have you seen the Glory? Have you been satisfied in it? Then you will share it.

Preach the gospel, die, and be forgotten.[10]

Forever worship the God of all joy with the saints and the angels.

The cost will be great. The reward will be greater. See the glory. Share the joy. Look and live.

8

Glory and Suffering

When you get to heaven, you will not complain of the way by which the Lord brought you.

John Newton

Keep runnin', keep runnin'
Don't lose heart, don't you give up now
Don't turn around
You've got to find a way somehow (to)
Keep reaching, keep fighting
The pain cannot compare to the reward
That will be yours, that waits in store
For those who just keep runnin'

On this road, this fight for holiness
I've struggled and I've bled . . .

"A Pilgrim's Progress"
from the *Look & Live* album

Imagine you were taken from your family, taken from earth, and dropped off on a distant planet. The atmosphere of this planet is not the same as earth's, and therefore every breath you take is cold and painful.

You are told that somewhere on the planet there is a ship that will take you back home, but you have to find it. The people who kidnapped you say that you have one year until your lungs collapse. They board their ship and leave.

You are baffled. The ship could be anywhere.

As you begin scanning the horizon, you notice boils are popping up on your skin. Breathing is becoming more difficult. Your bones ache as you walk.

You begin your long search.

Now, if you had been dropped off on a planet where the geography and atmosphere were like that of Costa Rica, you would certainly still be motivated to get back to home, but you would not be *as* motivated. Right? On "Planet Costa Rica," you might get distracted from your mission. You might be more inclined to nap.

But in this place, it would be impossible for you not to spend your every waking minute fighting to find that ship.

The pain and suffering, while it is frustrating and unbearable, has proven to be a source of wakefulness for you—a loyal, tangible reminder that you are not home. That you must get home. That your joy . . . your treasure . . . are someplace else.

For all the blood, sweat, and tears that suffering ushers into our lives . . . for all it robs from us . . . for all its misery . . . it is really a gift, especially for the believer.

I do not say those words lightly.

I know that some reading this right now have experienced terrible atrocities, and perhaps are experiencing them right now.

Know this: I hurt with you, and more importantly, God hurts with you. I do believe that death, disease, disaster, deep disappointment are bad things, awful things that God hates, and we should hate, too. But what I hope to show in this chapter, what I hope will fill your sails with hope, is that they are not ultimately bad things. They are the bitter medicine of a good physician. The slow, dissonant crescendo exploding into a blissful climax.

Especially for the believer.

Suffering Comes From the Father

First, I feel the need to briefly address an elephant in the room.

The Bible teaches that God is both sovereign and good, so why is there suffering? This is a serious problem for the mind, and has been for centuries.

The problem of pain (or problem of evil) is essentially this: If God allows suffering to be, then He might be sovereign but He can't possibly be good. In this case, He is just an all-powerful, evil dictator unleashing pain in our lives.

Or, on the other hand, if God allows suffering to be, then He might be good, but He can't be sovereign. In this case He wants the very best to happen for us, but He's simply incapable of achieving it.

The Bible teaches us that God is sovereign *and* good, and our experience teaches us that pain is real. Therefore, we need a category of thought that goes something like this: God can will things to be (in an ultimate sense) that He does not like (in an immediate sense).

Jonathan Edwards termed this "extended beauty" and "confined beauty." Other theologians talk about this in terms of God's secret will and God's revealed will. Books have been written on this subject alone, but to give us a framework, let's look at this idea through a couple of biblical/theological themes.

First, *salvation*. The Bible teaches plainly that God "desires all people to be saved and to come to the knowledge of the truth" (1 Timothy 2:4 ESV). And yet, the Bible also teaches plainly in Romans 9:18 that "He has mercy on whom He desires, and He hardens whom He desires." He has predestined salvation (Ephesians 1:11; Romans 8:29), and only some are saved.

So which one is it? All or some? Is He good or sovereign? Yes.

God wants (in an immediate sense) for all people to be saved, and yet (in an ultimate sense) He has chosen only some.

Second, *the cross*. Judas betrayed Jesus, and this evil was inspired by Satan (Luke 22:3). But the Bible also says that Jesus was "delivered up according the definite plan and foreknowledge of God" (Acts 2:23 ESV).

So which one is it?

Yes.

God hates sin, and yet He allowed (or ordained) the greatest sin ever committed to occur.

Now let's look at this idea through the lens of suffering.

The most famous story in the Bible and perhaps in the world about suffering is the story of Job. Job is described in chapter 1 of his book as an extremely righteous and wealthy man, and then we read this . . .

> Now there was a day when the sons of God came to present themselves before the Lord, and Satan also came among them. The Lord said to Satan, "From where do you come?" Then Satan answered the Lord and said, "From roaming about on the earth and walking around on it." The Lord said to Satan, "Have you considered My servant Job? For there is no one like him on the earth, a blameless and upright man, fearing God and turning away from evil." Then Satan answered the Lord, "Does Job fear God for nothing? Have You not made a hedge about him and his house and all that he has, on every side? You have blessed the work of his hands, and his possessions have increased in the land. But put forth Your hand now and touch all that he has; he will surely curse You to Your face." Then the Lord said to Satan, "Behold, all that he has is in your power, only do not put

forth your hand on him." So Satan departed from the presence of the Lord.

Job 1:6–12

Many of us know the rest of the story.

Devastation gets unleashed in Job's life, and basically everything around him gets torn from him. All his livestock (his money) are killed along with his seven sons and three daughters.

What I want us to see here is this: God, in this instance of suffering, and in all instances of suffering, is *totally and completely in charge* (you might say "ultimately"), and yet we see that the suffering is not directly (or "immediately") God's idea.

He allows it.

Notice that Satan says, "Put forth Your hand now and touch all that he has." The suffering is Satan's idea, and God responds by saying, "Behold, all that he has is in your power, only do not put forth your hand on him."

In other words, God is not fighting with Satan. He is totally in control, and is simply letting out Satan's leash: "You can do this, but you can't do that, etc."[1]

God hates suffering, the Bible is clear on this, and yet He ordains it.

Okay. Maybe you say, "I get it." Nice doctrine, man. But still the bitter question remains, Why?

Why did my mom die?

Why did my car get stolen?

Why did my dream disintegrate?

Why did my child get cancer?

WHY?

We will never know the specific reasons why God allows the pain He does in our lives, but we can know what is behind our suffering and find an unshakable, incomprehensible peace if we look through the cross.

The cross assures us of God's love for us, which is the greatest thing we need in times of suffering.

We all know this.

When you experience deep hurt in your life, you don't need someone to preach to you. You don't need someone to try to fix you. You don't need answers. You need a shoulder.

Well, lean in.

At the cross we see a God who not only works for our good, but who also suffers for it. Bleeds for it.

Look at Him.

The Infinite Innocent, suffering in the place of the Barabbas race.

If you can see Him sweating blood in Gethsemane, screaming in agony on Calvary . . . for YOU . . . then you can find peace in your deepest suffering and hope in your darkest hours.

Why?

Because now you have a God who understands your suffering, not only by omniscience but by experience. This shoulder you are crying on not only sympathizes with your weaknesses but empathizes with them.

But not only this.

When we look at our suffering through the cross, we see that the God who ordered the greatest tragedy ever, for the greatest good, will order our every tragedy for our good.

Look at Him.

If He ordered a bloody cross for our eternal salvation, will He not order our every little prick and tear for our benefit? This is Romans 8:32's logic: "He who did not spare His own Son, but delivered Him over for us all, how will He not also with Him freely give us all things?"

Because of the cross, we can know that all trials we meet are for our good. They have to be.

As Tim Keller says, "The cross does not tell us what our suffering means, but it does tell us what it can't mean. It can't mean that God doesn't love us."[2]

The cross is where we get faith. And when faith meets a trial, it does not say, "God is not good." It says, "This is God loving me. Indeed, it could not be anything else."

If you can see Him, totally abandoned, crying "why?" for you on the cross, then you can cry "why?" to Him freely while knowing you are forever embraced.

As to daily occurrences, it is best to believe that a daily portion of comforts and crosses, each one the most suitable to our case, is adjusted and appointed by the hand which was once nailed to the cross for us. Everything is needful that He sends. Nothing is needful that He withholds.[3]

John Newton

Do you believe Newton?

If you stare at the cross long enough, if you let your eyes adjust, you will.

We will always ask "why?" when we suffer, but if we look through the cross, we can live without the answer. This is the bedrock of peace, hope, and joy in our suffering. The goodness of God.

If we don't get this, we will rot on the inside.

The Reasonableness of Suffering

Faith alone can *assure our hearts* that suffering is for our good, but we can also find some assurance for our minds if we study the world around us.

No one bridged the gap between philosophy and faith better than C. S. Lewis. His book *The Problem of Pain* is a masterful look at the existence of suffering.

"What do people mean when they say, 'I am not afraid of God because I know He is good'? Have they never even been to a dentist?" Lewis writes.

Lewis says something here we all know to be true—that just because a thing is good, it doesn't mean it's easy, pleasant, or enjoyable. He also made this clear in his NARNIA writings when he talked about the Christ-figure Aslan ("... of course He's not safe . . . but He's good").

Suffering is never enjoyable, but you might see that it is *reasonable*.

We could say it like this. For a surgeon to heal a man, he must first wound him. He must cut him to fix him. For a musician to master her instrument, she must sit in a practice room and play until her hands bleed. She must suffer.

Nelson Mandela, thrown into prison at a young age, was released from prison twenty-seven years later and became the president of South Africa. He ended apartheid. The prison *made* him. Suffering made him the man he was—him and countless other heroes in history.

We see this in relationships: A relationship that has been battle-tested with arguments and annoyances is deeper and stronger than a "perfect" relationship.

We see it in anatomy: A bone that has been broken and healed is stronger than a bone that has never been broken. How does a muscle get stronger? It must be stressed. It must suffer.

We see it in music: Resolution is sweeter after the dissonance. *Because* of the dissonance.

Need I go on?

The way that God has made the world screams this: Redemption is better than perfection! There is a beautiful reason for our pain—a purpose for our trials—and that purpose is glory (Romans 11:36).

If God created the world, and we believe He is all-wise, all-powerful, and good, then we have to believe suffering is not a mistake. We have to believe it is better for pain and evil and suffering to have existed than for them not to have existed.

If God created us, and we believe He is all-wise, all-powerful, and good, then we have to believe *our* suffering is not a mistake. We have to believe it is better for pain and evil and suffering to have existed *in our lives* than for them not to have existed.

But we doubt God. We writhe in our pain and curse Him.

Lewis explains this well when he says we want "not so much a Father [in heaven] but a grandfather in heaven. . . ."[4]

Meaning this: Grandfathers give kids whatever they want. They just want the kids to *like* them. Fathers give their kids what they need. And sometimes that means a spanking. Sometimes that means saying no.

Sometimes that means suffering.

Suffering Exposes Our Treasure

I heard a pastor say once, "You will never really understand your heart when things are going well."

This is true.

Suffering, like nothing else, shows us what we really love.

Imagine with me: You are asleep in your house. Suddenly three guys break in, demand all your money, torch your house in flames, and then drive away with your two family cars. All that's left is your family in your driveway.

This would be awful.

However, imagine if the week before you had been given the keys to a mansion in Maui. This would lighten the blow a bit. Now you have something—a house—to "fall back on."

What do you "fall back on" when life crumbles?

That is your true god. That is what you are looking at.

When we suffer, we will always either: (1) Despair because our treasure was taken from us; or (2) "Fall back on" that which is our true treasure.

Think about this in the story of Job.

When Job suffered the loss of essentially everything, he was deeply saddened but still had his joy.

Why?

He still had his treasure. God was his source of identity and happiness, and suffering showed that.

Compare this to some modern-day Jobs. Earlier in this book I mentioned the Wall Street executives of 2008, several of whom committed suicide when the stock market crashed.

Why did they kill themselves?

Suffering stole their treasure.

When something we love is torn from us, it is always painful. But if the thing torn from us was our god . . . it will not be merely painful. It will be absolutely devastating.

Let me make this clear: It is good to grieve. Nothing is respectable about religiously stuffing our emotions. Notice that Job was honest . . . he tore his clothes and wept. But often the line between worship and idolatry is the line between sadness and despair. Consider these words from Paul:

> We are afflicted in every way, but not crushed; perplexed, but not despairing; persecuted, but not forsaken; struck down, but not destroyed; always carrying about in the body the dying of Jesus, so that the life of Jesus also may be manifested in our mortal flesh.
>
> 2 Corinthians 4:8–11

In suffering, God is always doing the tender, merciful work of exposing what is truly precious. This is painful, but is a gift.

Suffering awakens in us the truth of God's permanence over the frailty of creation. It sobers the soul inebriated with idolatry and opens the door for reality.

In suffering, God is doing the work of a surgeon. He is cutting us to heal us. He is giving us the bitter medicine that will heal us of our idolatry. Suffering is a gift because suffering is God's way of helping us keep a loose grip on this world.

I have said it before, but I will say it again: The reason God commands us to love Him with all our heart is not because He is an egomaniac! It is because He knows that anything we love more than Him will betray us. Eventually, we lose it by its death . . . or ours.

The enemy of joy is not suffering, it is idolatry. In this fallen world, suffering is really the servant of joy, because in suffering, our hands are ripped from the shadow and are now able to grasp the reality.

Now God, who has made us, knows what we are and that our happiness lies in Him. Yet we will not seek it in Him as long as he leaves us any other resort where it can even plausibly be looked for. While what we call "our own life" remains agreeable we will not surrender it to Him. What then can God do in our interests but make "our own life" less agreeable to us, and take away the plausible source of false happiness?[5]

C. S. Lewis

Suffering Deepens Our Beauty

The second reason we see that suffering is a gift is intricately related to the first one: Through suffering, God is making you, forging you, into a breathtakingly beautiful being.

He is putting you in the fire, bringing to the surface the idolatry dross—and then removing it.

This, too, is a bitter gift.

Nobody likes being a means to an end. We all want to be loved and appreciated for our own sake.

If you're just being nice to me because you need a charity project, that is not kind, it is insulting. I want to be valued because I'm valuable, not because you need a bigger spiritual résumé. If you're just being friendly with me because I'm influential and I can help get you a promotion or get you higher on the world-ladder, we aren't really going to be friends.

A friendship is built on conversation and mutual respect, not on sales pitches, not on awkward moments where we finally get to your real agenda.

In true friendship, just talking *is* the agenda.

I think sometimes we forget that God is a person—a person who deserves at least as much respect as we do, and of course, infinitely more. But I say "at least as much as we do," because we don't even reach that standard.

We use God to make ourselves look more charitable to others—to appear more humble—but really we're not humble, we're thinking about how humble we are. He's just a badge to us.

We use God when we pray. We never talk to Him just for the sake of talking, and we don't worship Him as an end in itself. We awkwardly assert our true agenda. We say to Him, "Okay, this is actually why I'm here . . ." And then we rant on and on about our real treasure. The sad part is, if we treat God this way, we will always treat people this way.

Follow this logic: If we use God—the One who is holy, uncreated, infinite, eternally valuable, and worthy of being loved for His own sake—how much more will we use people, the ones who are unholy, created, and finite? Infinitely less than God?

If we will step on an author, we will step on his books.

So what is the remedy?

Suffering.

Suffering is God's way of making me into a person of love.

If I never suffered, I would always have my fill of worldly desires. I would be a spoiled brat. I would always be using God to get to something less. I would always be using people.

I would be a predator, not a person.

I would always be distracted by the insignificant, rather than devoted to the magnificent.

But suffering is breaking me, slowing me down, humbling me. It is interrupting my pride—interrupting my agenda that was dreadfully off-kilter. And this is why it is good that we suffer, and also actually good that we do not understand the reasons why we suffer.

If we understood the reasons why we suffered—if, for example, I learned that I'm experiencing this painful thing because it's preparing me for something that will happen ten years from now—I wouldn't really have to love God for His own sake. I could still confide in my circumstance. I could still have some ultimate goal that is not Him.

But if I suffer and don't know why, if I serve God and get nothing out of it, if bad things actually come from it, only then can I know that I am loving Him for His own sake.

Love is the beauty of the soul. Suffering is bitterly painful. And it is making you breathtakingly beautiful.

Consider this famous passage of Scripture—one of my favorites—Psalm 27:4:

> One thing I have asked from the Lord, that I shall seek: That I may dwell in the house of the Lord all the days of my life, to behold the beauty of the Lord and to meditate in His temple.

Ah, yes. Here is David, loving God for His own sake. All David wants is God and a clearer sight of Him. He is happy and totally at peace, because his heart is fixed on the happiest and most peaceful Being in the universe.

Do you know what the context of this verse is?

Pain.

Armies are chasing David. Enemies are surrounding him. And he wants God?

Or consider this Scripture: "O God, You are my God; I shall seek You earnestly; my soul thirsts for You, my flesh yearns for You, in a dry and weary land where there is no water" (Psalm 63:1).

David is surrounded by deserts in this passage. He is physically thirsty. I don't know about you, but I'd be praying, "God, give me a well or something, please!"

But no . . . "My soul thirsts for You."

David's physical thirst awakened his true thirst—his soul thirst. The little ache woke up the big ache. His suffering made him dig deeper into his true joy. As one commentator put it,

"There was no desert in his heart, though there was a desert around him."[6]

That is what we need. And that is what suffering gives us.

A lot of us have the notion that our pain and trials are sort of dulling our joy—that they are really slowly killing us and our passion.

Actually, quite the opposite is true.

It is our prosperity that is killing us. Numbing us. Blinding us.

Prosperity is harder than pain because prosperity blinds us to our real need: a clearer sight of God. It distracts us from what will bring us real joy: seeing His face.

Suffering wakes us and makes us into people who are able to love and enjoy others for their own sake.

But not only this.

Through suffering, God is making me into a person of indomitable joy and unshakable peace. I don't know about you, but the people I am drawn to like a magnet are those who are the same no matter what is going on in their lives.

They are steady.

If all hell is breaking loose, they're somehow smiling.

If they strike success, become an overnight sensation, their smile is no bigger than it was before. They're the same person. There is something magnetic about this.

And this is why we suffer. Jesus wants to make all of us into this kind of person. God doesn't want us to be up and down, up and down. He wants us to be childlike in our faith, not in our attitudes.

Jesus is better than anything that prosperity can give, or anything that suffering can take. When your joy is in Him, the biggest trial doesn't shake you, and the biggest break doesn't make you.

When our eyes are on Jesus, when we live in His embrace, prosperity cannot add to our joy and suffering cannot subtract from it. As John Newton said, "When the Lord has put us in the possession of the pearl of great price, the gain or loss of a pebble is hardly worth a serious thought."[7]

How do you know you're becoming like Jesus? You can carry a cross and still have joy, and you can sleep like a baby in the middle of a storm.

Where do these fruits of the Spirit come from? They come from abiding in Jesus, and abiding in Jesus means suffering.

> I am the true vine, and my Father is the vinedresser. Every branch in me that does not bear fruit he takes away, and every branch that does bear fruit he prunes, that it may bear more fruit.
>
> John 15:1–2 ESV

He prunes.

Suffering and disappointment for the child of God are not optional. They are essential. God will always tear away from us what is harmful to us. God will challenge and test in us what is good for us.

Massaging the Gospel Into Your Suffering

Suffering is always polarizing.

As the saying goes, you get bitter or better. You lean into God and your soul gets bigger, deeper, or you lean away from God, into something else, and your soul shrivels.

This is why it is so crucial to know how to respond to seasons of suffering.

In all of our trials, enemy forces of doubt are sneaking into the camp of our hearts. In waves. They seek to destroy the truth, not with aggressive, courageous, face-to-face combat, but with the cowardly supplanting of lies.

They come in the night, with that age-old hissing, "God is not good." "He is not kind." "Look at your circumstances."

They deceive the warriors of truth into fighting an imaginary struggle, an internal battle of doubt, while the real battle rages on and the enemy forces advance.

So what do we need to do?

We need a watchman to chop off their heads.

And we certainly need this all the time in life, but we especially need it in seasons of suffering. We must be watching and waiting for the doubts to invade, and we should have a weapon in our hands ready to fight.

When I have personally experienced seasons of trials, I have found that this requires intense focus. I am continually listening to my heart, continually paying attention to how it is responding to difficult situations.

I'm listening for whether my heart is getting jaded, saying, "Well, here we go again," or "That's par for the course." Or I'm listening if my heart is saying, "Father, your plans are better than my expectations" or "I trust you, Lord."

If I am hearing more of the former than the latter, I have some work to do. Some killing to do.

The enemy is doubt (doubting the goodness of God), and the weapon we use, of course, is the gospel. But it's about more than just saying to ourselves, "Jesus died for you. Cheer up." The gospel should be *applied* to our suffering, massaged into our suffering.

And this, from my experience, requires a threefold attack. We have to tell ourselves *what could be*, *what is*, and *what will be*. All three.

Sometimes just using one of these approaches will leave the doubt whimpering but still alive, and will leave my heart still in a circumstance-focused despair.

First, when we suffer, we have to tell ourselves *what could be*.

When I suffer I must remind myself that no matter what I am suffering, I am never suffering as much as I should be. Hell is really what I deserve. Right now. I should be underneath the full weight of God's wrath and fury. For eternity. And I am not.

Let it settle.

It should have been me on that cross.

Let it settle.

This is the first stab. This is the first thing that gets the eyes off the circumstance and the hands off the entitlement.

When we compare the wrath of God with whatever our problem is, the problem will get infinitely lighter if our view of God is what it should be. The problem is real, the pain is hard, but what could be worse than "the wrath of God" abiding on you (John 3:36)?

Nothing.

The worst thing that has ever happened to you is not some difficult circumstance. The worst thing that has ever happened to you is *you*.

I am not making light of your circumstance. I am making heavy God's glory. You have sinned against I AM, the devastating realities of which cannot be surpassed by anything. The real trial you were destined for is the trial of His wrath—the trial that makes your current one seem like a stroll on the beach.

But, see, you are not in that trial! (Test your heart. See if there is surprise.)

Who is?

Jesus.

Look at Him. A man of sorrows, acquainted with grief. See Him there in Gethsemane . . . sweating blood, preparing to undergo your trial.

Behold! What manner of love is this?

See Him as they flog His body and imagine whose body should be there instead. Yours. Mine. Though He has never sinned, He is meeting God's wrath. And though you and I have always sinned, we are meeting His mercy.

See Him on your cross experiencing your agony and see that He understands your suffering. Not by omniscience but by experience.

We have to tell ourselves *what could be*.

But, second, we also have to tell ourselves *what is*.

What is real right now about my pain and suffering cannot compare to what is more real right now about the gospel and all its benefits. No matter how deep the pain is, a clear, warlike articulation of the gospel can always eclipse and outweigh whatever I am enduring. Of course, this is not necessarily immediate, especially if the pain is deep.

So what is? There are so many glorious things, but let me name a few.

Because of Jesus and what He has done . . .

I am established, anointed, and sealed by God (2 Corinthians 1:21–22).

I have been delivered from the domain of darkness and transferred to the kingdom of the beloved Son (Colossians 1:13).

I am loved by God, who gave himself for me (Galatians 2:20).

My old self has died, and my life now is hidden with Christ in God (Colossians 3:3-4).

I am God's chosen one, holy and beloved (Colossians 3:12).

I am forgiven (Colossians 1:14).

I am set free (Galatians 5:1).

I was chosen in Christ before the foundation of the world (Ephesians 1:4).

I was predestined for adoption through Christ (Ephesians 1:5).

I am dead to sin and alive to God in Christ Jesus (Ephesians 2:5).

I have been brought near to God by the blood of Christ (Ephesians 2:13).

I am a fellow citizen with the saints, and a member of the household of God (Ephesians 2:19).

I have received mercy, and the grace of Christ overflowed for me (1 Timothy 1:14).

I have received a kingdom that cannot be shaken (Hebrews 12:28–29).

I get to share in suffering as a good soldier of Christ Jesus (2 Timothy 2:3).

I have been granted by God's divine power all things that pertain to life and godliness (2 Peter 1:3).

I am known by God (1 Corinthians 8:3).

I am called a son of God, and so I am (1 John 3:1).

I am born of God, and therefore I overcome the world (1 John 5:4).

I am adopted by God, and by the Spirit of His Son my heart cries, "Abba! Father!" (Galatians 4:6).

I am no longer a slave but a son, and if a son, then an heir through God (Galatians 4:7).

I am released from the law to serve in the new life of the Spirit (Romans 7:6).

I am not condemned because I am in Christ (Romans 8:1).

Who shall bring a charge against me? I am God's elect (Romans 8:31).

I am more than a conqueror through Christ (Romans 8:37).

I will never be separated from the love of God in Jesus Christ my Lord (Romans 8:38–39).

I am confident that He who began a good work in me will bring it to completion (Philippians 1:6).

I am all these things, right now, no matter what I am facing. No matter where I am, I am seated with God in the heavenly places (Ephesians 2:6).

The way I comfort and gladden my daughters when they're brokenhearted, when they didn't get to go to the zoo or the pool, or they get a boo-boo, is not by focusing on their pain. I don't just say "it's okay" or "maybe there will be another time, sweetheart," or "it'll get better." I guide them into a different pleasure. "Look here . . ." "Let's do this . . ." "Think about this . . ."

Just last night I was walking onto a stage to lead worship, the last thing I wanted to do. I was downcast. It's been a hard year for the Papas—a miscarriage, loads of sickness, loads of uncertainty, wave after wave of unusual disappointment. But there I was on the stage. Everyone looking at me, waiting to be led. And so I sang . . .

> How rich a treasure we possess in Jesus Christ our Lord
> His blood our ransom and defense, His glory our
>   reward
> The sum of all created things is worthless in compare
> For our inheritance is Him whose praise angels declare[8]

I started to sing before I felt like it. I sang before I had a song. And I can't really describe it now, but I actually felt a load lifting. A joy rising. I've sung these words so many times before, but now the hammer of truth was pounding like a kick drum on my despair. *Do you believe this, Matt? Do you?* And a warrior hope was resurfacing. I began screaming for survival on the inside. *This is true! This is true! This is what is!* And I felt my soul breathe again. I looked, and I lived.

So count your blessings, as they say. Really count them. Count your spiritual blessings and count your earthly blessings, too. Tell yourself what is. Every day. Let your eyes adjust. And outweigh your boulder of suffering with the mountain of the love of God.

Suffering Produces in Us a Glory

We cannot only tell ourselves what *could be* or *what is*. We have to tell ourselves *what will be*.

> For momentary, light affliction is producing for us an eternal weight of glory far beyond all comparison . . .
>
> 2 Corinthians 4:17

Paul is saying here that the Christian's experience of pleasure to be had one day with Jesus will be so great, so heavy, that the heaviness of the trials and disappointments and despair of this life will feel like an ant bite. It will feel like a dream. The reality of delight in the presence of God will outweigh every heartache and every temporal joy on our journey. Put Jesus on one side of the scale, earth on the other, and the earth flies up.

208

I have heard this text preached often, and most of the time the pastors highlight this whole "outweighing" truth very well. But what I have never understood and never heard a pastor talk about is this: How does my suffering *produce* a weight of glory?

"For momentary, light affliction is *producing* for us . . ."

What's the deal with that? Isn't the Glory already going to be there? Should I hope for more trials here so that heaven will be better?

Here's my best shot at it.

One day, most likely (Lord willing), my daughter Paisley will walk across a stage and receive a diploma. She will be a high school graduate, and that will be an awesome day. It will be an accomplishment that any bystander in the audience would see and be happy for. Way to go, kid.

But her parents.

Her parents will be in snotty tears. Why?

Because they changed her diapers. They wiped her bottom a thousand times. They carried her from the car seat to her bed on late nights, and carried her through Disney World after she crashed out. They paid for her countless outfits and animals and lessons and hobbies. They have more invested in her than anyone else in the world.

The "afflictions" of parenthood served to "produce" a weight of glory in her graduation day, far beyond all comparison.

Or here's another way . . .

Daniel "Rudy" Ruettiger's life dream was to play football for the Notre Dame Fighting Irish. There was only one problem: he was a runt. He always got picked on playing tackle football as a kid. He told everyone his dream, and they would always laugh at him. Even his dad and his brothers would laugh.

When he came of age, his grades weren't even good enough to get him into Notre Dame. But he fought. He went to a junior college and studied his head off. Eventually, he got into Notre Dame.

He trained and trained, and he tried out for the football team. It was embarrassing. The guys hitting him were three times his size. But he kept getting back up. There was such a will and determination in him that the coach, out of sympathy, let him be on the B-team.

Long story short, in Rudy's senior year, in his last game as a college football player, he was standing on the sideline where he always stood. His dad and brother, whom Rudy had won over by his hope and resilience, were in the stands. The clock was winding down, and a chant began from the sidelines: "Rudy, Rudy."

Rudy had never played a single snap in a single game. He had only been a practice dummy.

Well, in the final seconds, the coach was won over. He put him in.

And wouldn't you know it, in the last play of the game, Rudy made the game-ending tackle. The crowd erupted. He was carried off the field a hero. It was a magnificent moment for everyone.

But for Rudy, for his dad and his brother, it was much more. There were blood, sweat, and tears in this moment. There were years of practice and study. There were lonely days when he wanted to give up the dream. He had more invested in this moment than anyone.

All the "afflictions" that he faced as a child and as B-squad runt served to "produce" a weight of glory, far beyond all comparison.[9]

This is what heaven will be like for us. Trials and tribulations on this journey are continually doing something for us, and that is this: They are deepening our appreciation of God over this world.

Every trial that comes, every cross we have to bear, is a chance we have to dig ourselves deeper into our true Joy.

He is worth it. He is better. He is good.

Keep going. Keep believing.

We don't need health. We don't need wealth. We need God. And then, at last . . .

We see Him.

And the pain is forgotten. We have our Treasure. And He is better.

Do you see it?

Heaven will not only be great in spite of all that we suffer. It will be great *because* of all that we suffer. Our afflictions are serving to produce our glory.

Remember, glory is about importance.

A thing can have objective importance, and a thing can also have subjective importance to you. You might (subjectively) consider something important that is not actually (objectively) important, or you might consider something (subjectively) not important that is actually extremely (objectively) important.

This is heaven: The objective importance of God—His glory—which is fixed, and the subjective importance that suffering has caused us to feel about God, colliding in a moment, for all eternity.

The most glorious experience imaginable.

Ever heard this phrase before? "Absence makes the heart grow fonder."

Ah, the infamous idiom.

Absence is suffering. Suffering makes the heart grow fonder.

This is why there is a narrow road. This is why there is a journey, a cross to bear.

A fonder heart for God.

This is why sin exists and pain exists and evil exists.

The finish line will be sweeter because the race was harder.

The resolution will be sweeter because there was dissonance. The hero will be greater because there was a villain. The glory will be greater because of the affliction.

Because.

For momentary, light affliction is producing for us an eternal weight of glory far beyond all comparison (2 Corinthians 4:17).

The Vision of His Face

As we have said *ad nauseam*, it is a sight of the glory of God that changes us (2 Corinthians 3:18). Our entrance into Christianity, also called *justification*, comes by a vision of glory. Our progress in Christianity, also called *sanctification*, comes by a vision of glory.

And so, what else would our final perfection in Christianity, also called *glorification*, come by, except a vision of glory?

First John 3:1–2 tells us this.

See how great a love the Father has bestowed on us, that we would be called children of God; and such we are. For this reason the world does not know us, because it did not know Him. *Beloved, now we are children of God, and it has not appeared as yet what we will be. We know that when He appears, we will be like Him, because we will see Him just as He is.*

Did you see the word *because* there?

"We will be like Him, *because* we will see Him just as He is."

What is the reason for our becoming like Him? Our seeing Him—the same thing 2 Corinthians 3:18 has been telling us all along. But this time, the vision is different. Now we are seeing Him "just as He is."

Did you hear what I said?

Just. As. He. Is.

Theologians for centuries have called this the "beatific vision," but we don't need to get lost in the theological jargon now.

Right now, just imagine it. Tell yourself what will be. Right now . . . in the midst of your disappointment and pain and hurt and loss and tragedy. Think. Believe.

His face is coming.

You've been squinting for so long—beholding, as in a mirror, the glory of the Lord. The road has been hard. It's been a slow and steady climb, looking through this broken *imago Dei* glass.

You've had victories and you've fallen on your face. The blur and the fog have been thick at times and you have lost your way.

You have followed distraction and been dismayed. But the taste . . . oh, the taste . . . these glory-glimpses along the way proved to keep you going. In the race.

Slow and steady, on the chase.

What kind of glory is this?

That these broken glimpses should captivate? That feeble glances my life would change? Who is this King of glory?

Move on with haste now, my soul, toward this embrace. For now we see through a glass dimly . . . but then, face to . . .

FACE.

And *therefore* . . .

Changed.

Completely.

Doubts erased.

Idols replaced.

Soul at rest.

Forever.

Not a phase.

Forever.

Sight.

No more faith.

Finally. Realized. Satisfied.

Gaze in one place.

Changed.

Behold, I tell you a mystery; we will not all sleep, but we will all be changed, in a moment, in the twinkling of an eye, at the last trumpet; for the trumpet will sound, and the dead will be raised imperishable, and we will be changed. For this perishable must put on the imperishable, and this mortal must put on immortality.

1 Corinthians 15:51–53

This glory-sight will change you. As it did at the start, when you first saw His glory and the sight saved you, gave you eyes of faith—faith to behold His glory. So will it be, on that day when you look full in His face, when you behold His glory with no impedance, no obstacle.

The sight itself will give you new eyes.

What kind of glory is this?

The sight itself will give you new eyes to see Him and enjoy Him forever.

Jesus' prayer will finally be answered: "Father, I desire that they also, whom you have given me, may be with me where I am, to see my glory" (John 17:24 ESV).

Imagine it.

You will never lust again.

Why?

Because you will see Him just as He is.

You will never envy again.

Why?

Because you will see Him just as He is.

You will never overwork again.

Why?

Because you will see Him just as He is.

You will never insult another human being ever again.

Why?

Because you will see Him just as He is.

You will never hoard your money again.

Why?

Because you will see Him just as He is.

You will never doubt God's love for you ever again.

Why?

Because you will see Him just as He is.
You will never worship creation ever again.
Why?
Because you will see Him just as He is.
You will never be sad ever again.
Why?
Because you will see Him just as He is.
Hallelujah.

There we shall see his face, And (therefore) never, never sin!
There, from the rivers of his grace, drink endless pleasures in.[10]

Isaac Watts

So take heart, dear one. You can make it through whatever you're going through. Tell yourself what will be.

As a musician, I've sung and played in a lot of weddings over the years, especially when I was just out of college. It seemed like back then I was playing in a wedding almost every weekend. I enjoyed those times, but to be honest, it got old pretty quick, especially dealing with sour, nitpicky wedding coordinators (I promise I'm not bitter).

Anyway, the moment that always kept me watchful and hopeful was the big moment . . . when the bride came down the aisle. It was never boring and was always worth the price of dealing with the wedding coordinator.

But really, the best part about it was never the bride. Don't get me wrong, a bride on her wedding day is almost always stunningly beautiful.

It was him.

The face of the groom was always my favorite thing to watch.

Giddy smile. Big masculine tears. Quivering lip. Melted heart. Love, beholding its beloved. Beaming. Radiant.

It always broke me more than anything.

One day, when this whole thing here ends, the bride of Christ is going to walk down the aisle of time, and we are going to see Jesus . . . and He will see us . . . and *His face will beam with joy.*

That is what will change us forever.

The look of delight on His face.

Giddy smile. Quivering lip. Eyes that tell a story.

Granted, we will be a stunning sight—beautiful beyond recognition. But it will not be because of our efforts. It will be because He washed us with His own blood. It will be all *because* of that look on His face.

It's coming.

You're going to see His face. His shining face. What rapture will this be?!? What ceaseless delight? Have you felt His love on this earth? Have you seen glimpses of His goodness *here*?

I want to pray along with you now with these longing lyrics from Ray Palmer (1808–1887):

> Jesus, these eyes have never seen,
> That radiant form of Thine;
> The veil of sense hangs dark between
> Thy blessèd face and mine.
>
> I see Thee not, I hear Thee not,
> Yet art Thou oft with me;
> And earth hath ne'er so dear a spot,
> As where I meet with Thee.
>
> Like some bright dream that comes unsought
> When slumbers o'er me roll,
> Thine image ever fills my thought,
> And charms my ravished soul.
>
> Yet though I have not seen, and still
> Must rest in faith alone;
> I love Thee, dearest Lord, and will,
> Unseen, but not unknown.
>
> When death these mortal eyes shall seal,
> And still this throbbing heart,

The rending veil shall Thee reveal,
All glorious as Thou art.[11]

So tell yourself *what could be.*
Tell yourself *what is.*
Tell yourself *what will be.*
And meet your suffering with a joy that all hell cannot shake.
Meet your storm with an anchor in your soul. He will never
let you go.

9

Show Me Your Glory

Among the lofty peaks and summits of man's prayers that rise like mountains to the skies, this is the culminating point.

Charles Spurgeon

I'm crying "more" from the depths of me
I want You, Lord, more than anything
I breathe again 'cause I live to see
Your glory, God
I caught a glimpse and it set me free
And now I know that the only thing
That could be better than what I've seen
Is what's in store
'Cause there's always more

"More"
from the *Look & Live* album

The alarm clock goes off. I should lift my heavy cranium. Snooze. Ten minutes of bliss. More loud noises.

The present is becoming the future at a steady rate of sixty beats per minute, whether I like it or not.

This is the moment . . . what it really all boils down to. What I've been gabbing about the last eight chapters.

Will I choose social media or my *New American Standard*?

Will I listen to the noise or the still, small Roar?

This is the moment.

Hit my feet or my knees? Email or Jesus? Work or Jesus? Finish this book I'm working on or Jesus?

An eternity of difference.

As high as the heavens are above the earth.

Now.

Choose this day. This moment.

God or gods. Creator or creation. Bread or crumbs.

Jesus or boredom. Worship or die.

Maybe I'm being too dramatic. I don't think so.

This moment contains all moments.[1]

C. S. Lewis

Theology is practical: especially now.[2]

C. S. Lewis

What comes into our minds when we think about God is the most important thing about us.[3]

A. W. Tozer

Do you believe all this? Do you believe the most important thing for you to do is to fight to get a real vision of God?

Sure, I get it . . . it's just another day. But is it really?

I'm reminded of what C. S. Lewis once said about Tolkien's epic story *The Lord of the Rings*.

I've never met Orcs or Elves—but the feel of it, the sense of a huge past, of lowering danger, of heroic tasks achieved by the most apparently unheroic people, of distance, vastness, strangeness, homeliness (all blended together) is so exactly what living feels like to me.[4]

Me, too, Jack. I feel it. There is an epic battle raging . . . an invisible war . . . a battle for my soul and the souls of men.

Every day. Now.

And I hear voices in my head, desires, some lulling me to sleep and some telling me to fight. Some numbing me to kingdom dreams and some telling me to jump on the front line.

The louder ones—the evil, more enticing ones—allure me not with pleas to fight on their side, but with notions of leisure. Lust. Video-game pursuits while real arrows whiz past my head.

"Everything will be all right. Relax," they say.

But the quieter ones—the true ones, the Gandalf-like voices in my head—tell me, "Everything will be all right. *But not yet.*"

I heard John Piper say once, "I wake up in the morning with Satan sitting on my face."

This resonates with me. A lot.

I don't wake up in the morning with overwhelming, affectionate feelings for Jesus. I just don't.

I wake up to noise. A familiar cacophony of emotions and inclinations. That loyal companion I affectionately call Desire. Sehnsucht. It begins as a swell. Anxiety. Deadlines pressing. Doubt.

What am I doing? Regret.

Where I should be by this time. Envy.

Look at where they are. Restless. Longing.

Random-fire, rapid-fire arrows.

The swell is surging.

Social media is calling.

Emails are pinging. Kids are waking.

O. My. God.

Matt's early-morning soul = chaos.

Now, when I feel that old wave surging—that animal of longing inside—I've got to rein that thing in, or I'm through.

Dead.

I've got to run downstairs and put my face in my Bible or I will live distracted. Discontent. Disappointed. If I don't tame the beast, I will live as Pascal said it in his *Pensées*, seeking diversion.⁵ Bouncing from thing to thing . . . going from 40-watt idol to 40-watt idol until my life is wasted.

I need an anchor. I need a center.

I need a Glory.

Your First Minutes

One of my favorite quotes is by a man named George Mueller, the nineteenth-century orphanage-builder and preacher. In his tract *Soul Food*, he writes:

> I saw more clearly than ever *that the first great and primary business to which I ought to attend every day was, to have my soul happy in the Lord.* The first thing to be concerned about was not, how much I might serve the Lord, how I might glorify the Lord; but how I might get my soul into a happy state, and how my inner man might be nourished. For I might seek to set the truth before the unconverted, I might seek to benefit believers, I might seek to relieve the distressed, I might in other ways seek to behave myself as it becomes a child of God in this world; and yet, not being happy in the Lord, and not being nourished and strengthened in my inner man day by day, *all this might not be attended to in a right spirit.*⁶

What Mueller is saying here is absolutely simple and absolutely revolutionary. He will not, or rather cannot, attend to his life in "a right spirit" if he does not first "have his soul happy in the Lord." That is his "first great and primary business."

Why?

Because in the first thirty minutes of your day, you are really setting the trajectory of your life. Get your soul happy in God because, as we know, the soul will be happy in *something*.

I have four lovely ladies in my life, my wife and our three daughters, and each possesses a thing I call a "love tank." Their love tank is basically their emotional, relational center (their heart) that I, as a husband and a dad, try to fill every day.

I do this by talking and listening. Tickling and kissing. Flirting and dancing.

Now, because my daughters are so young and emotionally expressive (that's a really nice way of saying *dramatic*), on days when their love tank does not get filled, you usually know it. Everyone does. They're grouchier. They're more attention hungry than usual.

They will basically do anything to get attention, which usually involves the loudest noises you can possibly imagine, dangling from my neck like a monkey for hours on end, and various degrees of inhumane behavior, in general.

This is cute, but actually it gets ugly as it matures.

What is a teenage girl who wears skimpy "clothes" and throws herself at loser guy after loser guy? She's just a girl who didn't get her love tank filled. She needed attention from Dad, and sadly, she didn't get it. She's starving.

And that is us when we don't wake up in the morning and look and live. We need attention from Dad, and if we don't run to Him who is always ready and waiting to give it, we will throw our souls at anything.

Let me show you how this works in my own life.

When I wake up and don't spend time with Jesus—when I don't "look and live"—I go out into the world in weakness.

I need people to say nice things about me, and when they don't, I get my feelings (my pride) hurt. I work really hard. Too hard.

I work anxiously, hysterically even. So I need things to happen "right this instant," and when they don't, I blame someone who works with me, or yell at them.

I envy others who have more success than I do.

I take myself way too seriously. Since a default idol of mine is success, when I don't behold Jesus, that's where my heart tends to go.

On the other hand, when I wake up and I get my soul "happy in the Lord"—when I get my "glory tank" filled by beholding Jesus—I go out into the world in strength. I have a center now.

If people say rude things about me, it might sting a little, but it hits my shoulder and bounces off.

I work hard, but it doesn't feel anxious. It doesn't feel like "everything." Work is not my identity—it's just me playing in God's giant sandbox. I have fun, I get done what I can, and then I go to bed.

I can celebrate others successes because I am secure in who I am.

I don't take myself so seriously because I take God as seriously as possible.

We all have a "glory tank" that we must fill with a vision of God every day, or we will throw our souls at anything.

We are wired to get attention from Someone, and the gospel is where we find this happy, overwhelming, soul-satisfying attention. In the gospel we learn that we are held in the highest regard by the highest being in the universe. In this gospel we hear the blessing our souls have always longed to hear: "You are my beloved son (or daughter), in you I am well-pleased."

Eclipse the Idols

Early on, when I was explaining the idea of this book to my wife, she said to me with a confused look, "So, is your book essentially about telling people they need to read their Bibles and pray?"

My answer, proudly, was "Yes!"

Honestly, I would beware of any Christian book that offers you a better-life-solution different from this one.

With that simple purpose stated, however, my aim in this chapter will be more practical, and specifically twofold: (1) to encourage you with all that is happening when you open your Bible, and (2) to encourage you with the posture in which you should open your Bible.

First, to show you all that is happening.

When we crack open our Bibles in the morning, we are doing more than a mere "quiet time." Dawn is breaking. God is saying in our soul, "Let there be light." We are beholding the glory of the Son of God, and *we are changing*.

Again, 2 Corinthians 3:18: "But we all, with unveiled face, beholding as in a mirror the glory of the Lord, are being transformed. . . ."

In this moment, we are seeing the Glory we were made for and being changed . . . on the spot.

Becoming more like Jesus on the spot.

Our souls are being satisfied. Hunger being filled.

Here in this moment, our idols are being eclipsed. Replaced. For now we are seeing the real Thing. All pseudo and cheaper beauty is being naturally pushed aside in the vision of this One.

Here we are putting ourselves on the better "diet." We are training our desires to love what is good, to enjoy the finer music.

Here we are giving our soul-arrows the bigger target.

In this moment, we are seeing the Treasure in the field that is worth selling everything for. In this moment. This is it. Here. Now. Look and live.

This is why Corrie ten Boom famously said, "Have an appointment with the Lord, and keep it." This is why having a time with God is so crucial. We are training our desires.

But secondly, and perhaps more importantly, I want to encourage you with the posture or way in which you should come.

How We Come

Why do you read your Bible? Why do you pray?

Have you ever thought about these questions? Because why

you do something is just as important, if not more important, than what you are doing.

When I was in college, I took a music appreciation class. I was a music major, but the class was a required elective for all students . . . which meant that the class was a delightful mixture of music and non-music majors.

Now, I absolutely loved the class. Are you kidding me? A class where all you do is listen to clips of music greats like Brahms and Bach and Liszt? Where someone taught me their ideas and methods?

But many of the students did not feel the same way.

Many were there to just get the grade, and get out. They were there to pass tests, *which totally changed the way they would listen to the music*. They didn't enjoy it, they endured it. Bach's *Mass in B Minor* sadly became a means to an end. Some were there for girls or socializing. Some were there to raise their hand and exert their wit. Some were there to dominate the test scores.

The irony is this: The people who were there simply to enjoy the music were the people who were the happiest, and the ones who actually made the best grades. (Yeah, I did that.)

Do you see?

We were all required to be there, but to some people it "felt required." We all listened to the music, but only some of us heard the music.

This is our problem when we read the Bible.

We are like an immature college freshman in music appreciation.

Our "why" is dreadfully off. We're not coming to feast, we are coming just to get through. To pass a test. To get on to our "real life."

We are just adding to our spiritual résumé. Check. Doing our duty.

The ineffable Word of the Lord tragically becomes a means to our end. A lesser end.

So what is the right purpose? What is the "why"? The "end"?
To enjoy the Music.

The glory of God.

This is the reason we open our Bibles: "Show me your Glory."

This is why we pray. To see more of Him. To adore more of Him.

As one early church mystic put it, we read "to find more reasons to love and desire God."[7]

More reasons. That ought to be our purpose.

"Whether you eat, or you drink" or you read the Bible. Everywhere we look in the world, and everywhere we look in the Bible, we are supposed to be seeing Glory.

Finding reasons.

And recognizing this . . . having this as our primary motivation . . . changes everything. Suddenly, we begin to hear the music. We see Him on every page.

To enjoy Him.

If we read the Bible as a plan to check a box, then it will be just that. But if we read looking for the glory of God, it will be that. We will stay there. We will linger. We will figure it out.

As we open our Bibles, we must be aware of our "why."

But we also must be aware of our need—both of our need to see glory and of our need for God to show it to us.

We have to remember that we were hardwired for glory, and that seeing God's glory has something to do with our efforts, but more to do with God's Spirit. Our growth and our sight of God comes from the Holy Spirit opening our eyes.

"This comes from the Lord, who is the Spirit."

As I said in chapter 5, personal Bible study and prayer are the primary ways we behold Glory and thereby become more like Jesus, and so I want to say a few practical things about each of them here.

Beholding Him Through the Word

The Bible is a book, which means we can glean from it in many ways.

We can learn historical facts.

We can learn ancient literary techniques and devices.

We can learn about real people and their stories.

Because it is a spiritual book, we can gain knowledge, wisdom, and doctrinal clarity.

We can learn much about ourselves and how we should live our lives.

But the Bible is more than a book, and it is more than a spiritual book. It is the Word of God. "All Scripture is God-breathed." And this means the primary thing it is always doing is revealing Jesus Christ.

Consider the famous Psalm 19: 1–2:

> The heavens are telling of the glory of God; and their expanse is declaring the work of His hands. Day to day pours forth speech, and night to night reveals knowledge.

A beautiful psalm here about the glory of God.

David begins the psalm with six verses about the glory of creation, how creation displays the radiance of God. And then in verse 7, it seems David has a case of ADD:

> The law of the Lord is perfect, restoring the soul; The testimony of the Lord is sure, making wise the simple. The precepts of the Lord are right, rejoicing the heart; The commandment of the Lord is pure, enlightening the eyes.
>
> vv. 7–8

Um . . . okay, David. What does the law of the Lord have to do with the sky?

Everything.

This psalm is not about two things: God's glory and also the Bible.

228

It is about one thing: the glory of God. David is telling us here that we see it in the sky, but mostly, we see it on the page. The Bible is not a portrait; it's a window.

It is not wrong to come to the Bible to get doctrinal clarity. But it is wrong to come to the Bible *mainly* to get doctrinal clarity. That is idolatry. That is knowing God to sound smart.

It is not wrong to come to the Bible to get wisdom for your daily living. That is wonderful. But it is wrong to come to the Bible *mainly* to get wisdom for your daily living. That is idolatry—using God to get your best life now. You will never see Glory that way. You will never get outside of yourself that way.

So how do we do it?

A lot of people will make suggestions about the best ways to read Scripture. They will offer questions for you to ask as you read like: "Is there a command to obey here?" Or, "Is there an example to follow?" "Is there a sin to avoid?" These are all well and good, but they do not reach the heart of our glory hunger.

The best questions to ask first are always, "Where is the glory? What does this passage teach me about God?"

Yes, where is He? What is He like? I must know. Those other questions are not bad at all, and they must be asked, but they should not be asked first, or we might be seeking some other end (god).

The primary purpose of the Bible is to reveal Jesus.

Let me show you how this works for me. When I was growing up I would read passages like Psalm 15:1–3, which says:

> O Lord, who may abide in Your tent?
> Who may dwell on Your holy hill?
> He who walks with integrity, and works righteousness,
> And speaks truth in his heart.
> He does not slander with his tongue,
> Nor does evil to his neighbor,
> Nor takes up a reproach against his friend.

I would read a passage like this, and first think, *Okay! I can do this. I will walk with integrity and work righteousness. I will speak truth. Help me, Lord.*

But this way of reading the Bible only led me to despair.

Why?

Because I can't do it. I try and I fail. I was thinking about behaving when I should have first been beholding.

When we read the question "O Lord, who may abide in Your tent? Who may dwell on Your holy hill?" our first thought should be: *Jesus. He is the only One who truly can. The One who walks with integrity and works righteousness, who speaks truth in his heart . . . who does not slander with His tongue. Jesus is so beautiful. He is so holy. I could never dwell on the holy hill of the Lord if Jesus had not walked up the hill of Calvary. O Lord, I praise you. Please make me more like you.*

Do you see the difference between the former and the latter?

The desire for change in the former is totally rooted in human resolve, where the desire for change in the latter is rooted in glory-beholding worship.

Or how about a classic example of David and Goliath.

When I was growing up in church this passage was always taught the same way: David was a nobody . . . he simply served faithfully. Because of that, one day he got his shot. He slayed the giant, and if you're faithful to Jesus, you'll have big opportunities to slay the giants in your life, too.

Sound familiar?

If we are looking at this story for His glory, however, it will be utterly different.

We will see that Jesus is the true David, a nobody who served his Father faithfully for years. When the giant of sin had us Israelites cowering in fear and failure on the sidelines, Jesus stepped out without any armor or credentials and saved the day. He cut off the head of Satan and rescued us from certain defeat.

Now, there's glory.

Do you see the difference?

When we read the Scripture this way, we are obeying the writer of Hebrews and we are "considering Him." We are holding up the diamond of God's glory and turning it and turning it and turning it, seeing new facets of His goodness all the time.

Always discovering more, always finding more reasons to worship Him. And *this* is what changes us.

We don't read the Bible to finish. We read it to change.

We read it to see glory.

Consider these words from Tim Keller, which are a wonderful example for us to follow for our biblical interpretation practices:

Jesus is the true and better Adam who passed the test in the garden, a much more difficult garden, and whose obedience is imputed to us. Jesus is the true and better Abel who, though innocently slain, has blood now that cries out, not for our condemnation, but for acquittal. Jesus is the true and better Abraham who answered the call of God to leave all the comfortable and familiar and go out into the void not knowing wither he went to create a new people of God. Jesus is the true and better Jacob who wrestled and took the blow of justice we deserved, so we, like Jacob, only receive the wounds of grace to wake us up and discipline us. Jesus is the true and better Joseph who, at the right hand of the king, forgives those who betrayed and sold him and uses his new power to save them. Jesus is the true and better Moses who stands in the gap between the people and the Lord and who mediates a new covenant. Jesus is the true and better Job, the truly innocent sufferer, who then intercedes for and saves his stupid friends. Jesus is the true and better David whose victory becomes his people's victory, though they never lifted a stone to accomplish it themselves. Jesus is the true and better Esther who didn't just risk leaving an earthly palace but lost the ultimate and heavenly one, who didn't just risk his life, but gave his life to save his people. Jesus is the true and better Jonah who was cast out into the storm so that we could be brought in. The Bible's really not about you—it's about him.[8]

Beholding Him Through Prayer

Our prayers, almost more than anything else, reveal us. They will reveal our deepest desires and longings, because what archbishop William Temple said is true, "Your true religion is what you do with your solitude."[9]

In other words, what do you intensely think about when you don't have to think about anything? This is your real god.

When we're alone, our thoughts travel up to something like a prayer. Even when we are praying in the more Christian or proper sense, our hearts might be captivated with something other than God. In other words, *prayer is not the antithesis of idolatry.* Let me show you why.

Think: If the world could read your prayer journal, would God look like a genie or a treasure?

If God answered every prayer you prayed this week, how many new Christians would be added to the kingdom?[10]

These questions are very convicting because they are showing us what we truly desire.

We really don't want God or His kingdom. We want our kingdom.

We are using God to get to what we truly love. Our prayers are just the rubbing of a lamp. We are in a sense sacrificing God on the altar of our true god.

Our idolatrous prayers are like asking a diamond to give us a lump of coal.

I heard Tim Keller say once, "There is a kind of person who prays only when they're deepest concern is at stake." I have sadly been this kind of person.

What we are truly concerned about, we pray about. With passion. And when we pray this way, when we pray as God-using idolaters, we will always feel a twinge of disappointment in our relationship with God. We will always feel as if He is not blessing us, because idols always evade us. They are never enough. Idolatry breeds dissatisfaction.

So what do we do? Stop praying? Ask for less?

No, we ask for more.

Jesus taught us how to pray, here in Matthew 6:9–13 (NIV):

> Our Father in heaven, hallowed be your name,
> your kingdom come, your will be done, on earth as it is
>   in heaven.
> Give us today our daily bread.
> And forgive us our debts, as we also have forgiven our
>   debtors.
> And lead us not into temptation, but deliver us from the
>   evil one.

Notice where Jesus begins prayer.

He does not begin prayer with a long list of concerns and worries. He begins with God.

The greatness of God.

The goodness of God.

He is a Father, and He is in heaven now, reigning above all things.

Lift your eyes off of your idols and onto Him. Place your little life underneath the loving rule of His kingdom and the perfect design of His will.

Does this mean that we should never throw our concerns and worries onto God?

Absolutely not.

God wants us to cast our cares upon Him and to make our requests known to Him (Philippians 4:6). *But we should make it the regular practice of our prayers to acknowledge the glory of God first. To adore Him first. To submit to Him first.* Then make our petitions known. And there is an important reason for this.

Let me tell you how this works for me.

When I come to God in the morning and begin with a barf

of concerns, I go on and on about "all my problems" with a pulse of worry. I pray anxiously.

Really, I'm meditating on my problems. I'm beholding the glory of some other god, and venting my idolatry to God with a sort of pathetic self-pity.

I'm pouting, not praying.

At the end of these "prayer times," I feel a certain sense of peace, but it's not a deep peace. It's the sort of peace that you have after you get something off your chest to someone without a real relational reconciliation, without a hug.

On the other hand, when I choose to follow Jesus' model for prayer, things are very different and not-surprisingly better.

When I begin with His glory, my heart goes upward and my idols get smaller. My worldly concerns fade in the light of His beauty and holiness. I adore Him for His own sake. I get my soul "happy in the Lord."

And then, after I have worshiped, when I begin to make my requests, suddenly they aren't so life-and-death.

I can make my requests with a smile, knowing that everything will go the way my Father in heaven wants it to go. Many things become less important and many things become more important.

My prayers for His glory to be spread across the city and the nations become more urgent because I have personally seen it and been satisfied in it.

Changed by it.

I urge you to follow Jesus' prayer model for your prayer times.

A wonderful model that has been developed from the Lord's Prayer in Matthew 6 (and also Isaiah 6 and others) is the ACTS prayer model. It is a great one if you do not currently have any "train tracks" for your prayers. It goes like this:

A—Adoration. Focus your attention on the glory of God alone. Behold Him for His own sake. Listen to the music. Simply praise Him.

> In the year of King Uzziah's death I saw the Lord sitting
> on a throne, lofty and exalted, with the train of His robe
> filling the temple. Seraphim stood above Him, each hav-
> ing six wings: with two he covered his face, and with two
> he covered his feet, and with two he flew. And one called
> out to another and said, "Holy, Holy, Holy, is the Lord of
> hosts, the whole earth is full of His glory."
>
> Isaiah 6:1–3

C—Confession. In light of God's blazing holiness, what sins
do you need to confess and repent of?

> Then I said, "Woe is me, for I am ruined! Because I am
> a man of unclean lips, and I live among a people of un-
> clean lips; For my eyes have seen the King, the Lord of
> hosts."
>
> Isaiah 6:5

T—Thanksgiving. Thank God for all His demonstrations of
grace and mercy in your life, *especially the cross.*

> Then one of the seraphim flew to me with a burning coal
> in his hand, which he had taken from the altar with tongs.
> He touched my mouth with it and said, "Behold, this has
> touched your lips; and your iniquity is taken away and
> your sin is forgiven."
>
> Isaiah 6:6–7

S—Supplication. Ask God for any specific requests and needs
that you may have and ask Him to work powerfully in the
lives of others.

> Then I heard the voice of the Lord, saying, "Whom shall
> I send, and who will go for Us?" Then I said, "Here am
> I. Send me!"
>
> Isaiah 6:8

This is a wonderful model, but there are many others.

The point is, you need one, or your prayers will devolve into a scatter-brained mess of idolatry venting.

God wants more for your life than bigger success. He wants to give you himself. How could it be loving for God to give you what you've always wanted if what you've always wanted isn't Him?

> If you then, being evil, know how to give good gifts to your children, how much more will your heavenly Father give the Holy Spirit to those who ask Him?
>
> Luke 11:13

God is the blessing you've been seeking.

When David prayed in Psalm 27:4 (NIV), "One thing I ask from the Lord, this only do I seek: that I may dwell in the house of the Lord all the days of my life, to gaze upon the beauty of the Lord and to seek him in his temple," did he mean that was literally his only request?

No.

The psalms are full of desires and requests to be saved from enemies and to be helped in practical ways. David just meant that this was his overwhelming desire.

To behold God. Because He is the blessing.

So what do you want?

The ignition to your prayer life is your most overwhelming desires.

If your prayers aren't beginning with God, if your most overwhelming desire is not God, then put yourself on the better diet.

Pick up your cross, and learn to pray new prayers. Better prayers.

Frustration is the path to happiness.

Learn to desire the Feast that you don't currently want, and you may find that you begin to forget the poison you currently crave.

Beholding Him Through Meditation

Let me do my best to put one more practical tool in your tool belt for beholding the glory of God.

The Bible has so many wonderful things to say about meditation.

The word *meditation* has gotten a bad rap from its prevalence in both Eastern mysticism and Catholicism. From these world-view streams, we assume that meditation is ivory-tower stuff. Something weird that out-of-touch monks do. But it is actually an incredibly practical, blue-collar kind of Christian discipline that we all need to incorporate in our lives.

First let's look at the benefits of meditation. The classic passage on this is Psalm 1:1–3:

> How blessed is the man who does not walk in the counsel of the wicked, nor stand in the path of sinners, nor sit in the seat of scoffers!
>
> But his delight is in the law of the Lord, and in His law he meditates day and night.
>
> He will be like a tree firmly planted by streams of water, which yields its fruit in its season and its leaf does not wither; and in whatever he does, he prospers.

Notice in verse 1 the transitory, inconstant nature of those who do not meditate on the law of the Lord. They walk, they stand, they sit in the places of evil. While those who delight in God's Word are a tree "firmly planted" by streams of water. A redwood.

Water represents a life-source, and the tree is rooted there. Thus, the fruit always comes, not in every season—there are good times and bad—but it always comes.

When we abide in Christ (John 15) and His steadfast love for us, which is our source of life, His life will manifest itself through us in spiritual fruit eventually and inevitably.

Consider these benefits of Scripture meditation from God's Word.

You will understand the fear of the Lord. (Proverbs 2:5)

You will walk in the way of good men. (Proverbs 2:20)

You will find favor and good understanding with God and men. (Proverbs 3:4)

You will have long life. (Proverbs 4:10)

You will have good health. (Proverbs 4:22)

You will have good success. (Joshua 1:8)

You will have prosperity. (Psalm 1:2–3)

You will excel in wisdom and understanding. (Psalm 119:97, 100)

You will have victory over sin. (Psalm 119:9–11)

You will have victory over enemies. (Psalm 119:23)

You will have victory over temptation. (Matthew 4:4, 7, 10)

You will have victory over the devil. (1 John 2:14)

You will discover how to live. (Proverbs 4:4)

You will be Spirit-filled. (Colossians 3:16; Ephesians 5:18–19)[11]

Needless to say, meditation is important.

Okay, but what *is* meditation?

I have put meditation in this chapter after Bible study and prayer because meditation is something more than these two, and actually something in between the two.

Meditation is studying God's Word in God's presence.

It is the curious mining of the Scriptures to find more ammunition for worship.

Meditation is about looking for reasons. It is brainstorming in God's presence. Wrestling with God's Word in God's presence to behold God's glory.

Eugene Peterson states in his book *Answering God*: "The Psalms are a book of prayers, but they begin with an admonition to meditate on the Word of God. Why is this? Because meditation on God's Word is the doorway to real, fervent, focused prayer."

George Mueller talks about facing this problem personally in his autobiographical tract *Soul Food*, which I referenced earlier:

> Formerly, when I rose, I began to pray as soon as possible, and generally spent all my time till breakfast in prayer, or almost all the time. . . . But what was the result? I often spent a quarter of an hour, or half an hour, or even an hour on my knees, before being conscious to myself of having derived comfort, encouragement, humbling of soul, etc.; and often after having suffered much from wandering of mind for the first ten minutes, or a quarter of an hour, or even half an hour, I only then began really to pray.

See what was happening to Mueller?

There was nothing to guide his prayers. There was no truth there yet to lift his sleepy eyes. But then he discovered the glory and the art of meditation:

> Now I saw, that the most important thing I had to do . . . was to begin to meditate on the Word of God; searching, as it were, into every verse, to get blessing out of it; not for the sake of the public ministry of the Word; not for the sake of preaching on what I had meditated upon; *but for the sake of obtaining food for my own soul.* The result I have found to be almost invariably this, that after a very few minutes my soul has been led to confession, or to thanksgiving, or to intercession, or to supplication; so that though I did not, as it were, give myself to prayer, but to meditation, yet it turned almost immediately more or less into prayer.

For Mueller, prayer began to happen naturally as his eyes turned toward the Lord.

And that is the essence of meditation: *praying through the Scriptures.*

Many of the religious streams that emphasize meditation, even the Christian ones, are built on individual imagination. They say we should center ourselves and imagine God—behold him with your mind's eye—and then pray.

The problem with this is, What if what you are imagining is wrong? What if it's not the true God? That is the beauty of meditating on God's Word.

So how do we do it?

Let me say this: Meditation can (and should) happen on an ongoing basis (1 Thessalonians 5:17), but it should also be practiced in focused intervals of time. Psalm 1:2 encourages us to meditate day and night, which can be interpreted literally (morning and evening) or simply as "on a continuing basis."

As mentioned earlier, the Hebrew word for *meditate* comes from the word that means "to chew the cud."

A focused reflection and an ongoing reflection.

I want to offer you a few things to practice in your focused time of meditation, some of which are things I personally practice and some of which are the suggested practices of various godly men.

(Let me emphasize *suggested* practices. None of these things are meant to be "law," a burden, or the only way to do it! They are simply ways you can grow that have helped others. You can find your own ways, as long as they are biblical ways.)

Centering Yourself

The first practice of good meditation is a centering of yourself. This is a rich tradition in Catholicism.

We should begin our meditation times by asking for God's help since seeing God's glory is a work of the Spirit.

"[This] comes from the Lord, who is the Spirit" (2 Corinthians 3:18 NIV).

We should come needy, poor, even desperate.

Hearing the gospel or reading the Bible without the Spirit's help is like playing a Beethoven symphony for a deaf man.

Take a few minutes to ask for the Spirit's help, and pray Moses' prayer: "God, show me your glory."

Look and Live

The second practice is one I simply call "Look and Live."
This one was gleaned from Martin Luther's *A Simple Way to Pray*, a wonderful book that focuses on praying through the Ten Commandments and the Lord's Prayer. Luther encourages Bible readers (meditators) to ask two primary questions:

- What does the passage say about God?
- What does it say about me?

I remember these questions with the two words *Look* and *Live*.
When I meditate, I take a couple of verses at a time, sometimes more, sometimes less. I read slowly and say "Look and Live" over and over in my mind. *Look*, meaning, where is the glory? What does this passage show me about you, God? (And the "you" there is important because, remember, meditation is brainstorming *in God's presence*.)
I spend some time just "looking," and I write down my thoughts.
After I Look, I *Live*.
I read and pray, "God, what are you saying here about how I ought to live? What does this passage say about man, or man as he should be? What would my life look like if this truth dominated my thinking?"
I write down these thoughts.
After I've written these things down, I have a list of things to reflect on and pray through, which is wonderful.

Garland Prayer

And that leads me to another possible third practice of meditation, which is sometimes called garland prayer.
This technique is sort of a combination of the ACTS prayer model and Luther's model. The idea is you take the truths that you have gleaned, and then you pray through them: Adoration, Confession, Supplication.

For example, let's say the passage you were meditating on was Psalm 23. From your meditation, one of the truths that you wrote down was that God is a patient and gentle God. And so you pray *around* this truth:

Adoration—Gracious God, you are so patient with me. Slow to anger, rich in love. You do not treat me as my sins deserve. You are always gentle with me, a stupid, stubborn sheep. How could I ever deserve a Shepherd like you? Why do you always call for me with such a gentle voice? I am so unworthy. You are good, and I worship you.

Confession—Lord, I am sorry for when I am not patient and gentle with others. When I am harsh or impatient, I have forgotten the gospel. When I am rude, I have forgotten that I am the (forgiven) chief of sinners. I so often wander from your gentle, patient spirit into the fields of self-reliance, and I humbly ask for your forgiveness.

Supplication—Lord, sweeten my heart by your Spirit, and make me ready today to deal with others as you have dealt with me. Make me a man like you, with a kind of fierce gentleness. I pray for my wife and my daughters that you would give to them that quiet, gentle spirit that 1 Peter talks about. (Use this section to pray about any need you have in your life related to the truth at hand.)

Pray through all the truths that God taught you this way. Do you see how deep you can mine one verse, even one word, of Scripture? This is a wonderful way to see Glory, and I highly recommend it.

Now, let me offer you a few more simple meditation tools, since sometimes in certain verses or passages it can be helpful to have several different methods.

Memorize

This is always a surefire way to meditate on God's Word.

You would be surprised at how much more you can mine from a passage when you memorize it.

Memorize, memorize, memorize.

Be warlike in this. Be disciplined. Dare I say, legalistic. Because this is a really good thing, if your purpose is seeing God more, not winning arguments or impressing mere mortals.

Emphasize

Emphasize each word of a verse. Let me show you what I mean by looking again at Psalm 23:1.

First say, "The **Lord** is my shepherd."

Who is my shepherd?

My shepherd is Jesus Christ, the Righteous. My shepherd is the God of the universe who is present everywhere and is all-powerful. Why should I be afraid?

Next say, "The Lord **is** my shepherd."

It is true. It is more real than my feelings. He is my shepherd.

Next, "The Lord is **my** shepherd."

My shepherd! Me, the sinner. I am His and He is mine. If I wander off, He will come for me because He is *my* shepherd.

And, "The Lord is my **shepherd**."

He is a shepherd. Good Shepherd is one of His names. That means He is my protector and provider. That means I am a stupid sheep that needs daily attention. That means I do not add anything to Him, but He adds everything to me. (And so on, and so forth.)

Personalize

Remember that the Bible is actually real. Remember that the people in it were actual people.

Imagine yourself sitting next to the author. Imagine the black-and-white text until you see scenes and colors. Imagine what it means that God "makes" you lie down in green pastures.

Put yourself in the passage, in the story. Replace pronouns with your name. Replace characters with yourself.

"The Lord is _____ 's (insert your name here) shepherd."

Harmonize

This last one is a good one, and it's really not just for poets and artists.

The idea is to take the passage you're meditating on, or want to meditate on, and add an element of art to it. Set it to a melody. Paint it. Write a poem about it.

For a poet, like seventeenth-century poet George Herbert, conceiving and writing poems was a way of holding a glimpse of Christ in his mind and turning it around and around until it yielded an opening into some aspect of its essence or its wonder that he had never seen before.

This is meditation: Getting glimpses of glory in the Bible or in the world, and turning those glimpses around and around in your mind, looking and looking. And then taking that glimpse and expressing it in a way that had never been said before.

Herbert found, as most poets have (and many preachers), that the effort to put the glimpse of glory into striking or moving words made the glimpse grow.

The effort to say deeply what he saw made what he saw deeper.

The effort to put the wonder in unexpected rhyme, or a pleasing rhythm, or startling cadence or meter, or an uncommon metaphor, or surprising expression, or unusual juxtaposition, or words that blend agreeably with assonance or consonance—all this effort caused his heart to see the wonder in new ways.

TRY IT.

Paul tells us that singing helps the word of Christ to dwell in us richly (Colossians 3; Ephesians 5).

Great art does this.

In the words of Francis Bacon, the job of the artist is "to deepen the mystery." Great art takes a truth in God's Word or God's world and makes it massive.

The artist meditates upon a truth until he sees it so clearly, and then he creates something to help others see what he has seen.

But really the wonderful thing about creating art is, in the process, you're helping yourself see.

I have given you a lot of tools here.

My hope is that you would find some that work for you and use them to behold the glory of God. That's why I wrote this book.

Don't read the Bible to finish, read it to change.

The Linchpin of Our Lives: Our Vision of God

Our beliefs, worldviews, and values shape us. They determine the choices we make, the friendships we keep, the careers we pursue, virtually everything about us.

The age-old sentiment is true: our thoughts become beliefs, beliefs become actions, actions become habits, and habits become lives.

You don't become Martin Luther King, Jr., or Adolf Hitler overnight. It takes years of thinking, believing, acting, and forging values . . . forging you.

Again, as A. W. Tozer said, if what comes into your mind when you think about God is the most important thing about you, the most important thing to do in your life is to get an accurate vision of God.

Get a vision of God that is bigger than the universe. Put the Lord in front of your face. Every. Day. Or you will fear everything but Him. You will love everything but Him.

> As it is, they cannot get quit of their old affections, because they are out of sight from all those truths which have influence to raise a new one. They are like the children of Israel in the land of Egypt, when required to make bricks without straw—they cannot love God.[12]
>
> Thomas Chalmers

245

Cannot love God. Have you ever felt this way? Do you feel stuck? Do you feel your heart cannot love God? Then give it something to love. Show it something magnificent. Open your Bible in the morning and hear God say, "I will make all my goodness pass before you." Quiet time? Ha. This is a soul eclipse. A soul embrace. This is everything you've ever wanted or ever needed. This is the glory of God in the face of Christ.

But remember Paul's words: "This comes from the Lord who is the Spirit" (2 Corinthians 3:18 NIV). No glory-seeing will happen apart from the Spirit's illumination. Period. So we should come desperate.

God, I need to see you. Need to see you. Open my eyes.

Then we should believe that we will see. We *will* see. We should believe that God gives good gifts to those who ask. And what better gift is there than a vision of His glory? God loves to make the poor rich. The broken whole.

The only prerequisite for grace is knowing you desperately need it.

Tomorrow morning you're probably going to wake up. And when you do, there will be a life-altering choice before you.

The Word or the world?

Jesus or Facebook?

Bread or crumbs? Life or death?

What will you choose?

The best advice I can give you: Look unto Jesus, beholding his beauty in the written Word.

John Newton

Make your life one unflinching gaze at the glory of God. This is why you exist. This is the only addiction that can finally set you free.

Behold the Lamb of God who takes away the sin of the world. Look and live.

Notes

Introduction

1. Daniel Levitin, *This Is Your Brain on Music* (New York: Penguin, 2007), 197.
2. John 1:23
3. John Newton, *Sixty-Six Letters: To a Clergyman and His Family* (Charleston, SC: BiblioBazaar, 2008), 85.
4. Blaise Pascal, *Pensées* (New York: Penguin, 1995), 209.
5. Timothy Lane, counselor and president of the Christian Counseling and Educational Foundation, used this phrase in his article "Godly Intoxication: The Church Can Minister to Addicts," *Journal of Biblical Counseling*, Vol. 26, Number 2, http://www.ccef.org/sites/default/images/JBC-26-2.pdf.

Chapter 1: Glory and Worship

1. Jonathan Edwards sermon (1734), "A Divine and Supernatural Light," http://www.monergism.com/thethreshold/articles/onsite/edwards_light.html.
2. Colossians 1:17 teaches us that Christ is presently holding all things together, and He certainly does not allow things to exist for no reason.
3. Other passages indicate the connection between glory and goodness that will be explored later. For example, if we read Genesis 1 and Isaiah 6 together we see that God made everything *good* and that the earth is filled with His glory. See also Psalm 33:5: "The earth is full of the lovingkindness [or goodness] of the Lord."
4. Charles Spurgeon sermon (1908), "A View of God's Glory," http://www.spurgeon.org/sermons/3120.htm.
5. Jonathan Edwards essay (1765), "The End for Which God Created the World," republished in John Piper's book, *God's Passion for His Glory* (Wheaton, IL: Crossway Books, 1998), 233.
6. *60 Minutes* interview, originally broadcast November 6, 2005, http://www.cbsnews.com/news/transcript-tom-brady-part-3/.
7. Timothy Keller, *Encounters with Jesus* (New York: Dutton, 2013), 28–30.

8. Harold Best, *Unceasing Worship* (Downers Grove, IL: InterVarsity Press, 2003), 19.

9. David Platt sermon, "We Glorify Christ," February 8, 2009, http://www .radical.net/media/series/view/2/we-glorify-christ?filter=series.

10. Ravi Zacharias, "Our Disappointments Matter to God," October 17, 2007, http://www.rzim.org/just-thinking/our-disappointments-matter-to-god/.

11. C. S. Lewis, *Mere Christianity* (New York: HarperCollins, 1952, 1980), 136–137.

Chapter 2: The Glory of God

1. John Piper, "What Is God's Glory?" www.desiringgod.org/interviews/ what-is-gods-glory.

2. John Piper sermon, "To Him Be Glory Forevermore," December 17, 2006, www.desiringgod.org/sermons/to-him-be-glory-forevermore.

3. I think I first heard this idea from theologian Michael Reeves.

4. Timothy Keller, *The Reason for God* (New York: Dutton, 2008), 214–215.

5. C. S. Lewis, quoted by Timothy Keller in *The Reason for God*. Originally found in *Mere Christianity* (New York: HarperCollins, 1952, 1980), 175.

6. The Canadian Encyclopedia, "Louis Cyr," http://www.thecanadianencyclo pedia.ca/en/article/louis-cyr/.

7. Space facts found at www.universetoday.com.

8. *The Physics Factbook*, "Length of a Human DNA Molecule," Glenn Elert, editor, http://hypertextbook.com/facts/1998/StevenChen.shtml.

9. R. C. Sproul, *Chosen by God* (Carol Stream, IL: Tyndale, 1986), 16.

10. Abraham Kuyper, inaugural lecture at Free University of Amsterdam (1880), http://www.reformationalpublishingproject.com/pdf_books/Scanned_Books_PDF/ SphereSovereignty_English.pdf.

11. Charles Spurgeon sermon, "God's Providence," No. 3114, October 15, 1909. http://www.spurgeon.org/sermons/3114.htm.

Chapter 3: Bad Aim (Glory and Sin)

1. J. R. R. Tolkien, *The Letters of J. R. R. Tolkien* (New York: HarperCollins, 2000), 110.

2. Timothy Keller, *Counterfeit Gods* (New York: Dutton, 2009).

3. Timothy Keller sermon, "Hell: Isn't the God of Christianity an Angry Judge?" October 22, 2006, http://sermons2.redeemer.com/sermons/hell-isnt-god-christianity -angry-judge.

4. C. S. Lewis, *The Great Divorce* (New York: HarperCollins, 1946, 1973), 71, 75.

5. A theme of Jonathan Edwards' essay, "Freedom of the Will," published in 1754.

6. Blaise Pascal, *Letters*, translated by M. L. Booth (New York: P. F. Collier, 1910), 354.

7. Blaise Pascal, *Pensées*, translated by W. F. Trotter (New York: Dutton, 1958), 51.

Chapter 4: The Blazing Center

1. John Donne sonnet, "Nativity," http://www.sonnets.org/donne.htm#003.

2. This idea is the theme of John Piper's *God Is the Gospel* (Wheaton, IL: Crossway Books, 2011).

3. Charles Spurgeon sermon, "A View of God's Glory," published November 26, 1908, http://www.spurgeon.org/sermons/3120.htm.

4. Timothy Keller, *The Freedom of Self-Forgetfulness* (Lancashire, England: 10Publishing, 2012), 39.

5. It should be pointed out that Benjamin Franklin's kite-lightning adventure makes a great story, but it probably isn't true. The legend is thought to be based on an article he wrote for the *Philadelphia Gazette* in 1752 that described a theoretical kite-flying experiment, http://www.discovery.com/tv-shows/mythbusters/mythbusters-database/ben-franklin-electricity.htm.

6. Charles Spurgeon sermon, "Contentment," May 25, 1860, http://www.spurgeon.org/sermons/0320.htm.

7. Timothy Keller sermon, "Removing Idols of the Heart," October 22, 1989, http://sermons2.redeemer.com/sermons/removing-idols-heart.

8. Stephen Charnock, *The Complete Works of Stephen Charnock*. I have updated the language in this quote.

Chapter 5: Let My Eyes Adjust

1. In *Unceasing Worship* (Downers Grove, IL: IVP, 2003), author Harold Best uses the metaphor of lemonade (pop music) and wine (classical music): Good lemonade is good, but good wine is better.

2. Herbert Simon, "Designing Organizations for an Information-Rich World," in Martin Greenberger, *Computers, Communication, and the Public Interest* (Baltimore, MD: The Johns Hopkins Press, 1971), 40–41.

3. Louis C.K. appearance on *Late Night with Conan O'Brien*, aired September 19, 2013. Reported at http://www.usatoday.com/story/life/people/2013/09/20/louis-ck-says-smartphones-are-toxic/2843185/.

4. Charles Spurgeon, *The Treasury of David*, Psalm 123 commentary (1885), http://www.spurgeon.org/treasury/ps123.htm.

5. A. W. Tozer, *Alliance Weekly*, June 3, 1950 editorial.

6. Henry Scougal, *The Works of the Rev. H. Scougal* (London: Ogle, Duncan, and Company, 1822), 22.

7. James K. A. Smith, *Desiring the Kingdom* (Grand Rapids, MI: Baker Academic, 2009). The quote here is from an interview with Smith, "You Can't Think Your Way to God," *Christianity Today*, May 24, 2013, http://www.christianitytoday.com/ct/2013/may/you-cant-think-your-way-to-god.html.

8. Martin Luther, *Table Talk* (1566).

9. C. S. Lewis, *Mere Christianity* (New York, HarperColins, 1952), 164.

10. A. W. Tozer, *Fellowship of the Burning Heart* (Alachua, FL: Bridge-Logos, 2006 edition), 82.

Chapter 6: Scattered Beams

1. Mike Mason, *Champagne for the Soul* (Vancouver: Regent College, 2003), 26.

2. It would be an overstatement to say that the people of these two views would never show any affection toward or interest in people (aka artwork) they did not like. I believe they would and do. However, we must say that since they do not know or admire the Artist as a starting point, if they do demonstrate some level of affection or interest, there will be a pulse of self-interest.

3. Timothy Keller's summary of Jonathan Edwards' observation in *The Nature of True Virtue*. Quote from Keller's *Generous Justice* (New York: Dutton, 2010), 182.

4. C. S. Lewis, "First and Second Things," *God in the Dock* (Grand Rapids, MI: Eerdmans, 1994), 280.

5. *Turn Your Eyes Upon Jesus*, words and music by Helen Lemmel, 1922, public domain.

6. John Owen, *The Glory of Christ* (Carlisle, PA: Banner of Truth, 1994), 7.

7. G. K. Chesterton, *Tremendous Trifles* (New York: Dodd, Mead and Company, 1910), 115.

8. Thomas Dubay, *The Evidential Power of Beauty* (San Francisco: Ignatius Press, 1999), 77.

9. G. K. Chesterton, *The Collected Works of G. K. Chesterton*, *Vol. 1* (San Francisco: Ignatius Press, 1986), 263–264.

Chapter 7: Glory and Mission

1. Charles Dickens' 1843 novel *A Christmas Carol*.

2. John Piper, *Let the Nations Be Glad* (Grand Rapids, MI: Baker Academic, 2010), 35.

3. C. S. Lewis, *The Great Divorce: Collected Letters of C. S. Lewis* (New York: HarperCollins, 2001), 85.

4. C. S. Lewis, *Mere Christianity* (New York: HarperCollins, 2001), 174.

5. Jonathan Edwards sermon (1753), "The Pure in Heart Blessed," http://www.biblebb.com/files/edwards/heart.htm.

6. Timothy Keller via Twitter, January 16, 2014, https://twitter.com/DailyKeller/status/423936779238899713.

7. Oswald Chambers, "The Unblameable Attitude," *My Utmost for His Highest*, http://utmost.org/classic/the-unblameable-attitude-classic/.

8. Story adapted from *History of the Moravian Church*, J. E. Hutton (Fort Worth, TX: RDMc Publishing, 1909, 2006), 228–232.

9. C. S. Lewis, *The Weight of Glory* (New York: HarperOne, 2009), 26.

10. Nikolaus Ludwig von Zinzendorf (1700–1760), a Moravian missionary better known as Count Zinzendorf, echoed the teachings of John Wesley when he said a missionary must be "content to suffer, to die and be forgotten." http://countzinzendorf.ccws.org/world/.

Chapter 8: Glory and Suffering

1. See Timothy Keller sermon, "Questions of Suffering," January 6, 2008, http://sermons2.redeemer.com/sermons/questions-suffering.

2. Ibid.

3. John Newton, *The Letters of John Newton to Mrs. Wilburforce* (London: The Religious Tract Society, 1869), 75.

4. C. S. Lewis, *The Problem of Pain* (New York: Macmillan, 1962), 28.

5. C. S. Lewis, *The Problem of Pain* (New York: HarperCollins, 2001), 94–95.

6. Charles Spurgeon, "The Treasury of David," Psalm 63, http://www.spurgeon.org/treasury/ps063.htm.

7. John Newton, *Letters by the Rev. John Newton* (London: Religious Tract Society, 1869), 84–85.

8. "How Rich a Treasure We Possess" by Matt Papa and Matt Boswell, on *Messenger Hymns* (Vol. I) by Matt Boswell, Doxology & Theology, 2012.

9. Daniel "Rudy" Ruettiger, http://www.rudyintl.com/truestory1.cfm.

10. Hymn, *Marching to Zion*. Words by Isaac Watts, 1707.

11. Hymn, *Jesus, These Eyes Have Never Seen*. Words by Ray Palmer, 1858.

Chapter 9: Show Me Your Glory

1. C. S. Lewis, *The Great Divorce* (New York: HarperCollins, 1946), 109.

2. C. S. Lewis, *Mere Christianity* (New York: HarperCollins, 1952, 2009), 155.

3. A. W. Tozer, *The Knowledge of the Holy* (New York: HarperCollins, 1978), 1.

4. C. S. Lewis, quoted in *The Collected Letters of C. S. Lewis, Vol. III* (New York: HarperCollins, 2007), 971.

5. Blaise Pascal, *Pensées* (New York: Penguin, 1995), 40.

6. Quoted in *Autobiography of George Müller: The Life of Trust*, H. Lincoln Wayland, ed. (Grand Rapids, MI: Baker Books, 1981), 207.

7. This quote has been attributed to Saint Peter of Alcantara (1499–1562).

8. Timothy Keller, "A Gospel-Centered Ministry," The Gospel Coalition conference, 2007, http://theresurgence.com/files/2007/06/26/20070626_gospel-centered-ministry_sd_audio.mp3.

9. Quoted by Timothy Keller, *Counterfeit Gods* (New York: Penguin, 2009), 168.

10. A question posed by J.D. Greear, "A God Like No Other" sermon, http://www.jdgreear.com/wp-content/uploads/2013/06/2e-4-Things-Only-True-of-the-Real-God-1-Kings-17-8-24.pdf.

11. Larry Wolfe, "The Blessings and Benefits of Scripture Memory/Meditation," Sermon Central, October 1990, http://www.sermoncentral.com/sermons/the-blessings-and-benefits-of-scripture-memory-meditation-larry-wolfe-sermon-on-disciplines-scripture-136696.asp.

12. Thomas Chalmers sermon, "The Expulsive Power of a New Affection."

Matt Papa is a minister and recording artist based out of Raleigh, North Carolina, where he lives with his wife, Lauren, and three daughters, Paisley, Stella, and Sofi. He serves as an artist-in-residence and worship leader at The Summit Church in Durham and is currently finishing a master's degree at Southeastern Seminary.

For over a decade, Matt has been singing, writing, and recording songs that are saturated with God's Word. To Matt, a song is more than just lyrics and melody—it's a sermon people will remember.

His album *Look & Live* is a loud and liberating call to people everywhere to break the chains of boredom, addiction, and idolatry . . . not ultimately by trying harder but by experiencing a greater thrill: the beauty and glory of God. At the heart of Matt's ministry is a vision to see the nations worship the one true God, and to that end, Matt radically leverages his life, his ministry, and his music. Learn more at www.mattpapa.com.